Digital Transformation of SME Marketing Strategies

Riccardo Rialti • Lamberto Zollo

Digital Transformation of SME Marketing Strategies

Innovating for the 4.0 Era

palgrave
macmillan

Riccardo Rialti
University of Milan
Florence, Italy

Lamberto Zollo
University of Milan
Milan, Italy

ISBN 978-3-031-33645-4 ISBN 978-3-031-33646-1 (eBook)
https://doi.org/10.1007/978-3-031-33646-1

This Palgrave Macmillan imprint is published by the registered company Springer Nature Switzerland AG.
The registered company address is: Gewerbestrasse 11, 6330 Cham, Switzerland

Contents

About the Authors

Riccardo Rialti, PhD is Assistant Professor of Management in the Department of Economics, Management and Quantitative Methods at the University of Milan (IT). Previously, he has been a Research Fellow and Adjunct Professor of Management at the University of Florence and an adjunct professor at Polimoda and IED institutes. He received a PhD in Business Administration and Management from the University of Pisa (IT) in 2019. He has been a visiting faculty member at the University of Lincoln (UK), Middlesex University London (UK), Sophia University (JAP), and ESCP Europe (FR). His main research interests are related to digital technologies for management and marketing. In detail, over the years, his research focused on big data, organizational dynamic capabilities, knowledge management and ambidexterity. His papers have been published in international journals such as *JBR*, *IEEE-TEM*, *TFSC*, *MD*, *BPMJ*, *CIT*, *BFJ*, *JGM*, and *WREMSD*. Recently, Riccardo also started to work as a strategic consultant for SMEs wishing to digitalize and expand their business.

Lamberto Zollo, PhD is Associate Professor of Digital Marketing and Innovation in the Department of Economics, Management and Quantitative Methods at the University of Milan (IT). His main areas of research refer to SMEs' new technology adoption and digital transformation, as well as marketing and managerial decision-making processes in startups and organizations. He has served on editorial boards and has published articles in several international peer-reviewed journals such as *Journal of Business Research*, *Journal of Business Ethics*, *Business Strategy & the Environment*, *Journal of Managerial Psychology*, *Technological Forecasting & Social Change*, and *International Journal of Production Research*.

List of Figures

List of Tables

1

Introduction

The last decade has dramatically changed the way businesses operate. Among the principal driving forces of change, technology represented the main force. The business world transitioned from a semi-analogic paradigm to a fully digital one. Businesses were then obliged to switch the way they were operating, including data among their core resources, and starting to rely on machine-based decisions.

This kind of change started during the third Industrial Revolution, during which computers started to assist managers and employees in the execution of most tasks. However, with the 2011 start of the fourth Industrial Revolution (Industry 4.0), the need for businesses to update has become a prerogative (Bagnoli et al., 2019). Adapting to compete with already existing Industry 4.0-compliant businesses required anyone else to change internal processes to include technologies. In particular, it emerged how computers embedded with artificial intelligence (AI) for big data analytics (BDA) were capable of dramatically enhancing business performance; thus, a run toward these technologies emerged (Huynh et al., 2020).

Production-side processes were the first to be affected. Internet of Things (IoT) availability (enhanced by advanced sensors, actuators, and

R. Rialti, L. Zollo, *Digital Transformation of SME Marketing Strategies*,
https://doi.org/10.1007/978-3-031-33646-1_1

tracking technologies) has provided businesses with the deepest-ever knowledge about operations and generated cost reduction and consequent revenue increases (Caputo et al., 2016).

Initially, marketing-side processes stuck with traditional procedures; indeed, social media, e-commerce, and digital platforms already provided huge mechanisms to connect with consumers and reach new markets. However, some of these Industry 4.0-oriented technologies have also started to prove fundamental in the marketing context.

For example, VR & AR, IoT, BDA, blockchain, AI, mobile technologies, and digital payments have all emerged as pivotal to improving traditional digital strategies (Krishen et al., 2021). Hence, managers started to exploit the potential of these technologies outside the production realm to improve marketing communication (i.e., using big data for micromarketing), to better promote products or brands (through VR or AR), to provide additional assistance to consumers (through IoT transmitting information about product status), to reduce counterfeiting or second-hand sales (by using blockchain to trace the authenticity of products) or by enabling different means of payment (Buhalis & Volchek, 2021). Additionally, Industry 4.0 technologies connecting marketing and production sides also proved fundamental for inventory management, as it was possible to monitor the production progress, how many products were available, and thus sell the right amount to the right consumers (or eventually by providing the correct information about the best-expected delivery). All these implementations defined the broader concept of I4.0-based Marketing, or Marketing 4.0.

Small and medium enterprises (SMEs) were initially laggards or late-comers in a rush toward Marketing 4.0. Usually, we refer to SMEs when talking about companies whose main objective is not fast growth or business model scaling, such as their mostly innovation-based counterparts, startups (Kirk & Zollo, 2021). Instead, we refer to companies having economic stability as one of the main goals, as well as a 'limited' number of employees (less than 250 in Italian law) and economic revenues (less than 50 million euros in Italy).

On the one hand, their larger counterparts needed more financial resources to invest in innovative technologies or a sufficiently skilled workforce to implement them. On the other hand, they hoped to have the data necessary to make the system work as expected. Technological evolution then came with their help. First, the possibility of depending on larger partners to develop technological solutions emerged. For example, providers such as Amazon or Google started to develop SME-tailored solutions that could be implemented through cloud-based services. Infrastructure thus became leaner, less expensive, and less human-dependent. Second, new production machines or inventory systems started to be embedded with sensors to collect data, and SMEs too initiated to have big data at their disposal for advanced analysis (Troise et al., 2022).

To the best of our knowledge, scant attention has been given by researchers and practitioners to the definition of a holistic framework capable of assisting SMEs in digitally transforming their marketing strategies in a 4.0 fashion (Aversa et al., 2021).

This book aims to guide SME managers wishing to implement such strategies. Our starting point is represented by the definition of the 'marketization' of the SME business model. Then, building on institutional theory, we attempted to define the path SMEs have to undertake to remain competitive in today's marketing arena. Insights were drawn from three exemplary Italian SMEs that successfully digitalized their marketing processes to achieve diverse objectives related to 4.0 technologies.

The second chapter then explores Industry 4.0 with a critical approach. It concludes with defining the most significant challenges that marketing managers will encounter in the 4.0 era.

The third chapter then focuses on the leading technologies enabling digital transformation, their importance first on the production side and then on the marketing side, and the main 4.0-based business models (Trento et al., 2018). A focus is then dedicated to the marketization 4.0 business model archetype.

The fourth chapter concentrates on how marketing strategies became consumer-centric thanks to technology. In doing so, the new generations of consumers and their behavioral habits have been described. After that, how big data and big data analytics have emerged as critical resources and key processes has been assessed. Then, new frameworks reassuming this phenomenon have been observed. Particularly, how SMEs could adopt or develop competitive intelligence tools has been conceptualized.

The fifth chapter provided the qualitative analysis and the selected cases' relevance to observe the phenomenon's evolution. Likewise, the results of our study are presented in this section.

The sixth chapter provides managers and marketers with a checklist to be implemented in the digital transformation of marketing in a '4.0-oriented way'. We offered insights about how it may be possible to observe the environment, understand the best solution, and implement it.

Finally, the seventh chapter will present the book's conclusion and provide an explicative graphical framework. Suggestions about potential future trends disrupting SME marketing strategies have also been provided.

Our book aimed to provide the most possible comprehensive way to deconstruct the phenomenon. Henceforth, we attempted to be as inclusive as possible regarding the industries in which our model could be implemented.

References

Aversa, J., Hernandez, T., & Doherty, S. (2021). Incorporating big data within retail organizations: A case study approach. *Journal of Retailing and Consumer Services, 60*, 102447.

Bagnoli, C., Dal Mas, F., & Massaro, M. (2019). The 4th industrial revolution: Business models and evidence from the field. *International Journal of E-Services and Mobile Applications (IJESMA), 11*(3), 34–47.

Buhalis, D., & Volchek, K. (2021). Bridging marketing theory and big data analytics: The taxonomy of marketing attribution. *International Journal of Information Management, 56*, 102253.

Caputo, A., Marzi, G., & Pellegrini, M. M. (2016). The internet of things in manufacturing innovation processes: Development and application of a conceptual framework. *Business Process Management Journal, 22*(2), 383–402.

Huynh, T. L. D., Hille, E., & Nasir, M. A. (2020). Diversification in the age of the 4th industrial revolution: The role of artificial intelligence, green bonds and cryptocurrencies. *Technological Forecasting and Social Change, 159*, 120188.

Kirk, N. H., & Zollo, L. (2021). *European Venture Toolbox: The path for SMEs to grasp and defend opportunities*. Emerald Group Publishing.

Krishen, A. S., Dwivedi, Y. K., Bindu, N., & Kumar, K. S. (2021). A broad overview of interactive digital marketing: A bibliometric network analysis. *Journal of Business Research, 131*, 183–195.

Trento, S., Bannò, M., & D'Allura, G. M. (2018). The impact of the 4th industrial revolution on the high-tech industry. *Symphonya. Emerging Issues in Management, 2*, 145–157.

Troise, C., Corvello, V., Ghobadian, A., & O'Regan, N. (2022). How can SMEs successfully navigate VUCA environment: The role of agility in the digital transformation era. *Technological Forecasting and Social Change, 174*, 121227.

2

SMEs' Digital Transformation from a Marketing Perspective

2.1 What Does Digital Transformation Mean in the Marketing Literature?

Companies today are rushing headlong to become more digital.
However, what does the expression 'digital technology' truly mean?

2.1.1 Internet, Computer, and Businesses. A Brief Overview

During the early 1960s, the United States Department of Defense endorsed the very first research on exchanging data in a binary-code format based on the existing networked telecommunication lines. The primary outcome of such studies was the development of the so-called ARPANET (a.k.a. Advanced Research Projects Agency NETwork), the earliest packed-switching-based computer network allowing users to exchange information with connected people quickly. According to

R. Rialti, L. Zollo, *Digital Transformation of SME Marketing Strategies*,
https://doi.org/10.1007/978-3-031-33646-1_2

computer science scholars, ARPANET represents the first successful use of an internet-based computer network (Mowery & Simcoe, 2002).

Throughout the first decade of its existence, the internet was restricted to US armed forces. Such a convenient way of exchanging information was indeed too crucial for national interest purposes to be shared with other partners. However, in time, studies about the internet approached an acceptable maturity level, and the US armed forces decided to start collaborations with American universities engineering schools to reap new ideas from universities researchers.

The opening of the internet to universities and research institutions was the first turning point in the history of computers and the Internet. Specifically, at that moment, businesses also started to approach universities to develop computer and internet-based technologies capable of improving day-to-day operations' efficiency and effectiveness. Original computers and internet-based technologies for industry were quite rudimental, with businesses focused on systems capable of storing, retrieving, and sharing information they already had in the chartaceous format more economically. The successful integration of these technologies into operations was fundamental to making the interest of civil society and the business environment grow enough to elevate computers and the internet to a global phenomenon status (Dickson, 2000). It was in the 1970s that the costs of computer or internet-based technology implementation were still so high that only the most prominent businesses of the time could afford to purchase the required hardware and train the workforce. In addition, telecommunication infrastructure was obsolete, and it could not allow the sharing of massive amounts of information. The benefits of integrating computers and the internet were tangible for the few users of computer-based and internet-based technologies. As such, businesses' attention toward these internet-based technologies increased, in parallel with private investments aiming to improve the existing technologies.

With the successful applications of computers and the internet and the consequent growth of R&D investments, during the 1980s, most large businesses were already relying on internet-based or intranet-based systems to run their day-to-day operations (Bousdekis et al., 2019). Consequently, computers and internet technology producers could finally achieve economies of scale due to increased demand; thus, computers became affordable for most businesses. In this vein, telecommunication services providers also started to upgrade infrastructures to allow the transmission of more significant flows of data.

The combination of these three factors, namely, (1) economies of scale in computers and systems production, (2) infrastructure adequateness, and (3) successful applications in prominent pioneers, was the spark that ignited the internet revolution of the 1990s and early 2000s. A revolution that is still going on, apart from a short period during the dot-com bubble of 2000–2002 (Ljungqvist & Wilhelm, 2003), still affects how traditional companies are doing business. Coherently, this twenty-first century we live in has been called the 'digital era'. Similarly, pertinent literature stressed how we outlived the third Industrial Revolution—or the computer and automation revolution—and we are now witnessing the dawn of the fourth, which will be the digital/cyber-physical systems led revolution (Kim, 2018). Although the third and fourth Industrial Revolutions are based on digital technologies, the third one was primarily related to computer-aided operations and integration of the internet into traditional ways of doing business to increase efficiency and effectiveness. The fourth Industrial Revolution is instead associated with the integration of 'intelligence' and 'cognition' into machines. Thus, during the third Industrial Revolution, human intervention was still fundamental to making devices and systems work. In contrast, the fourth revolution 'will give machines independence' to act independently and autonomously decide what needs to be produced and how to solve production-related problems.

Industry 4.0 may generate the most significant impact on companies' performance. Whereas in the third one, human skills represented the base for any technology usage and for the connection between different operation phases, in the fourth one, machines will autonomously interact with each other to develop total solutions to address different situations. Such a possibility offers enormously untapped potential in terms of optimization and organization (Bousdekis et al., 2019). Human work and decision making will, in fact, be highly augmented by the prospect of having more insights into processes. Machines can simulate almost infinite possible alternative solutions, evaluate the situation according to existing parameters, and consistently adapt the procedure to change. Managers of tomorrow may thereby affect all the possible combinations of their business at any moment from anywhere, relying on almost seamless computational capabilities from cloud-based platforms. Scenario-based analyses are becoming extremely simple, even in cases where IT skills are low. Additionally, managers may exploit machine-based decision making and optimization even if they perceive that they cannot solve a problem quickly due to missing information or data.

As imagined, operations are not the only impacted business process; marketing strategy formulation has also been affected. During the third Industrial Revolution, the power of the internet emerged in the marketing arena. However, the fourth revolution shows us how it is possible to target consumers at an unprecedented rate (Bagnoli et al., 2019). The more available data, the more information about consumers is in the hands of marketing managers. Additionally, many touchpoints are emerging over time, allowing marketing managers to contact new and unexpected consumers. Everything is also empowered by exceptional computational capacity, offering the possibility to imagine any different reaction on the consumer side (Marrucci et al., 2022).

The revolution is then continuing. Or, better, it has never stopped, and new strategies are needed for any business. Moving from these general considerations, this book will provide future managers with some guidelines to address the upcoming fourth Industrial Revolution in marketing management for SMEs (Small and Medium Enterprises). In particular, the text will focus on how to properly exploit existing technologies, reap benefits related to the digital environment, and get started with an innovative digital strategy. However, before starting the narration, some questions need to be answered, in particular:

a. *What was the meaning of the expressions 'digital' and 'digital technologies' during the third Industrial Revolution, and what will it mean in the following years during the fourth?*
b. *Are there any touchpoints in these definitions that are worth being considered?*
c. *Why did the expression digital and digital technology emerge as one of the most common jargons in day-to-day business language?*

2.1.2 The Expressions of Digital and Digital Technologies: How Do They Become Two of the Most Diffused Jargon in Management and Marketing Language?

The term digital originally derives from the Latin *digitus*, which means finger. The word is currently used to describe any technological device whose functioning is based on a two-digit or binary code. In fact, according to binary-code rules, the complexity of reality may be transformed into a sequence of 0 and 1 with the help of a computing machine. Then, this two-digit information can be transferred to another computing machine using an information infrastructure and decodified again into a meaningful message that a human user can understand. As any computer or information technology works this way, the term digital emerged as a commonly accepted prefix when someone has to talk about anything related to the internet or computers. Hence, digital technology arose as jargon to generically describe a technology based on computers and the internet. In more detail, digital technology can be identified as any computing machine and internet-based technology capable of allowing two users to exchange information as a binary-code message.

In the early stages of the third Industrial Revolution, the expression digital technology mainly was used to portray basic computer architecture. Thus, this expression was principally used to describe new technologies developed around microelectronics digital circuits instead of mechanical or analogic electronic circuits. This was true even in the business context.

During the late 1980s–early 1990s (when computer-based applications started to diffuse in any kind of business), the term started to gain additional meaning for businesses and managers. Specifically, in the timespan mentioned above, managers started to use the term digital technologies to refer to computers in the offices, often linked to a shared database, with software to perform specific tasks. The Internet was already fundamental, but due to the limited presence of web browsers and the scarcity of available information, it was mainly used to share data between two users (either within the same business or in two different ones) that already acknowledged each other's internet coordinates (i.e., IP address or email address). Internet Communication Technologies (ICT or IT) were rudimental, and even IT architectures—albeit complex for these times—were only capable of the essential functions (i.e., internal and external data sharing or data analysis), which was common to any Web 1.0 technology. This does not mean that the usefulness of this technology for the late 1980s or early 1990s companies was not significant, but indeed technologies' functions were restricted to particular uses. As an example, in this era, pivotal digital CRM tools emerged; thus, companies could seminally identify consumers' preferences using computers and categorizing their shopping behavior automatically (Peppard, 2000). Hitherto, the parameter to classify consumers was quite essential compared to today's standard, that is, businesses relied mostly on consumers' monthly expenditures or the products they acquired most.

Similarly, digital billing and accounting tools also emerged in this stage of computers and internet stories. Thus, businesses could register day-to-day accounting and financial data thanks to computers. This phenomenon not only allowed for improved management control (due to the possibility of using computers to identify mistakes quickly) but also fostered the appearance of business intelligence and enterprise resource planning (ERP) suite software. Data about sales, purchases, and resource utilization stored in a unique dataset (or in a special computer) offered the possibility for software developers to create systems capable of providing managers an overview of resource consumption or the state of current operations (Gbosbal & Kim, 1986).

The meaning of digital expression in the business context received additional significance with the Worldwide Web (WWW or Web) diffusion. The Web—a worldwide diffused information space populated by information explorable with the help of web browsers—offered businesses the opportunity to collect public information online. Hence, the Internet as we know it today was born with the birth of the Web. The diffusion of broadband internet infrastructure accompanied this; thus, digital technology was no longer only about the use of computers and limited networks to collect internal data and to share data with partners, but the meaning of digital technologies in business contexts also started to encompass the utilization of the internet as a tool. In particular, while talking about digital and digital-related opportunities, managers talked about internal networked systems capable of collecting and analyzing internal data while simultaneously being capable of accessing the internet and the information available online. In this moment, the Web 1.0 paradigm was replaced by Web 2.0, which is the web paradigm that allows users and businesses to interact online by creating web pages.

The Web (in this case, Web 2.0) was therefore another turning point for the meaning of digital in the business context (Andriole, 2010). The Web first offered businesses the opportunity to use online platforms for data elaboration and management (i.e., online free software). Second, it presented the opportunity to download extensions and upgrade existing software (thanks to open-sourced outdates or fully open-source software). This also allowed businesses to obtain customized software at meager costs. Finally, the web was the leading 'cause' of the birth of social media, which allowed companies to advertise to consumers using different strategies (i.e., social media marketing, social media communities, and message-based communications), and to gather an unexpected quantity of data about customers' feedback, product preferences and, in general, behavior (Kaplan & Haenlein, 2010).

In this regard, the transition from the Web 2.0 paradigm to Web 3.0 started to occur. While for long the expression Web 2.0 continued to be dominant in literature and practice, the specific shift initiated at the moment it became clear how the web could have been used as a consultable database. The marking line in such an evolution of the web was represented by the start of integrating artificial intelligence (AI)-based technologies in web applications. AI-based technologies enacted the possibility of identifying confidential information and information patterns within the web, thus allowing businesses to be flooded with exploitable information for different purposes. Similarly, worldwide internet infrastructure evolved to enable the transmission of unimaginable data quantities a few years ago. It was the first decade of this century, and this shift was also one of the causes of the start of the fourth Industrial Revolution, which paved the way for machines' autonomous interactions.

In this panorama, it was observed how an overall parallel paradigm shift occurred: Web 2.0 evolved into Web 3.0 (or Web3). This transformation of the web proved fundamental to enacting the overall transition.

Web 2.0 was based on social media, flat design of applications but responsive interactions, mobile technologies, content sharing, and big data and profiling tools (Trento et al., 2018). Web 3.0 is instead founded on virtual and augmented reality, blockchain, semantic web, spatial web tools, cloud-based artificial intelligence, and content creation (Table 2.1).

Whereas the transition between Web 1.0 and Web 2.0 was then mostly incremental, the change between Web 2.0 and Web 3.0 was radical. The advancements in web technologies then make it possible to advance the management decision-making process in an incomparable way. Managers frequently have more information than they can manage, so having at-d disposition tools to select the most relevant pieces automatically is fundamental. Likewise, marketers have so many channels at their disposal that selecting the most effective one could be extremely challenging without the help of artificial intelligence. The same could also help identify automatic actions that may be performed to improve business relationships with consumers. The internet-based interactions between consumers and businesses have never been so high. These technological trends initially were not the bread and butter of SMEs in terms of marketing strategies. However, with the decreases in usage cost caused by the increasing economy of scale by technology providers, in the short term, these

Table 2.1 Web 2.0 versus Web 3.0

Kind of web and macro characteristics	Web 2.0	Web 3.0
Enabling internet connection	*Mobile internet connections*	*Seamless internet connection*
Principal communication spaces (touchpoints)	*Social media*	*Virtual worlds (or virtual spaces)*
Enabling technologies	*Cloud computing with traditional algorithms*	*Cloud-based artificial intelligence, blockchain*
Targeted audience	*Community*	*Individual consumers*
Principal actions from consumers	*Content sharing*	*Content creation*
Analytical tools	*Big data/profiling tools*	*Semantic web/spatial web*
Application design	*Flat design but responsive design*	*Immersive 3D design*
Payment method	*Credit cards*	*Crypto currencies*

Source: Authors' elaboration

technologies will affect—as described in the successive chapters—the way SMEs operate significantly.

With the start of the fourth Industrial Revolution, the digital expression started to encompass all the meanings it has today. Specifically, in the current fourth Industrial Revolution, the word digital is used by managers and practitioners to describe any digital technology based on computer networks, capable of accessing the internet to extract information and endowed with analytics capabilities of analyzing data to identify existing patterns. In addition, digital technology is used to describe any technology characterized by AI capabilities, which allow computers to autonomously decide which information is more critical and determine which supply, production, or sales strategy is the best for businesses' efficiency and effectiveness (Chen et al., 2012). Examples of such digital technologies are predictive manufacturing systems based on computer-integrated technologies, which are systems based on computers deciding autonomously from humans involved in production (Xu et al., 2014). Similarly, modern digital technologies are extensive data analytics systems integrating web crawlers, which are technologies characterized by extracting unstructured digital data from online pages, analyzing them, and providing insights about trends occurring in the digital environment (Gandomi & Haider, 2015). Additionally, other current examples of digital technologies are tools such as 3D design tools, 3D scanners, and 3D printers, as they work with the help of computer networks and web-based software (Caputo et al., 2016).

Thus, as it was possible to observe, the meaning of digital expression (particularly the expression of digital technologies) has always been context- and time-dependent. However, its current purpose is significantly rooted in the fourth Industrial Revolution context. While originally digital was just used to describe anything that can be done with a computer, today it is related to many additional computer-based and internet-based (or web-based) technologies, each with a different potential use. The fourth Industrial Revolution, which is associated with the emergence of Web 3.0, is the most revolutionary element in the business environment over the last decades, and it contributed to shaping the world in the way we know it today.

Therefore, as the scope of this book is to explain to managers and practitioners how to deal with the *current* digital environment, we will build on the most inclusive definition of digital and digital technologies. Coherently, in the following paragraphs, the expression digital technology will regard any technology as digital based on computers, with data collection, analytic, and sharing capabilities, relying on the internet for its functioning, and characterized by AI capabilities. According to the perspective we will use throughout this book, these technologies may exist only in a purely digital or online form (i.e., a web crawler) or in a cyber-physical hybrid form (i.e., a production tool connected to the internet). This definition is remarkably similar to digital artifacts in the pertinent literature. It is possible to define a digital artifact as any artifact relying on a digital processor and the web to complete a specific task, either autonomously or with human intervention (Majchrzak et al., 2016).

As digital technologies may complete an almost infinite number of tasks and provide businesses with a huge amount of information, they can cause huge disruptions to the traditional ways businesses operate. The new information may provide evidence about how a conventional process is no longer efficient for current standards. Hence, while the new evidence may generate substantial competitive advantages for a business, it does not come without a cost, in this case, it disrupts the usual way of conducting day-to-day operations. Accordingly, companies must transform to exploit digital technologies. Such a transformative process is called digital transformation.

Moving from these premises (and keeping in mind the meaning we attributed to the expression digital and digital technologies), in the following paragraphs, we will first talk about the primary outcomes of the worldwide adoption of digital technologies, the causes of digital transformation, and how businesses may survive a digital transformation. Next, we will focus on the main topic of this book, how digital transformation affects current SMEs.

2.2 The Effects of Worldwide Diffusion of Digital Processes and Transformation for SMES

Digital technologies are transforming several physical processes or goods into digital ones. They are reshaping the real world progressively, as we can see from many examples, such as the possibility of exchanging information online replacing traditional physical documents. The use of smartphone applications has led to the replacement of several physical service providers, such as travel agencies, cinemas, and, to a certain extent, taxicab companies. E-wallets are replacing traditional ones, and electronic or digital money is replacing real money. Likewise, in contemporary environments, the current trend shows how consumers are increasingly willing to purchase digital products together or replace real-world products.

Just as any macro change affecting the real world will cause effects on businesses, digital technologies are also causing huge effects on businesses. Seven main effects of digital technologies on businesses have been identified. These seven effects of digital technology are digitization, disruption, dematerialization, demonetization, democratization, disintermediation, and decentralization (a.k.a. the 7Ds).

Regarding the academic exploration of the phenomenon, most extant literature has focused on observing how large businesses modified their business models to adapt to new technologies constantly emerging in the environment. This choice is quite intuitive whether we consider the original costs that businesses were experiencing to implement new technology and adapt to different contexts. In the earliest stages of the fourth Industrial Revolution, not only were technologies expensive, but extensive workforce retraining also required significant investments. Transformations in a digital fashion were also associated with cultural change projects that required long and burdening processes. However, in more recent times, SMEs are also progressively facing digitization, and it will be relevant to consider how they are approaching the most common problems and defining models that other SMEs may follow (Aversa et al., 2021).

Indeed, SMEs represent a vital component of any national economy. SMEs are the predominant kind of business worldwide; they are the principal employers in most countries, significantly contribute to national GDP growth, generate innovations, and are the backbone of global supply chains. Recent figures about SMEs show that they represent approximately 99% of business in China. In the US, more than 30 million SMEs exist (about 80% of the overall private ventures), generating approximately 40% of the GPD (Zollo et al., 2022). Likewise, in the UE-27 and UK, SMEs received the lion's share in economic effect at the national level. For example, in Italy, there are approximately 148,000 active SMEs in the 10–249 employee category, representing 92% of the companies operating at the national level (Troise et al., 2022). Such a figure increases whether micro-enterprises (1–10 employees' range) are considered (which account for another 6% of the total number of businesses). Approximately 15 million people work in SMEs in such a context. Similar numbers are also found in Germany and the UK. First 2022, there were approximately 2.6 million SMEs, and the vast majority were micro-sized enterprises; instead, SMEs *strictu sensu* capped at about 418,000 units. In the second context, about 5.5 million micro-enterprises and SMEs exist, with those employing between 10 and 49 people totaling approximately 389.000 units. About 16.2 million people in the UK work for an SME, and these businesses generate an economic impact in the 2.3 trillion-pound range.

Henceforth, while large companies are frequently the engine of most national economies, SMEs represent the fuel, making the machine run smoothly and obtaining better performance. SMEs are the fabric of economic tissue, enabling the existence of any global supply chain.

For these reasons, understanding and guiding SMEs into the transition toward 4.0 marketing is fundamental (Dash et al., 2021). SMEs are a completely different animal concerning large companies; they have informalized procedures, miss many departments, and often their decisions are concentrated in top management. The traditional literature is insufficient, and it is necessary to observe the effects of digitalization on these businesses in detail.

i. *Digitization*

As assessed in the previous paragraphs, any use of digital technologies is based on the exchange of some information. While information exchange always exists in the business context, digital technologies transformed most physical information or communication into digital information (Loebbecke & Picot, 2015).

The transformation of physical information into digital information occurred for the first time when businesses started implementing computer and internet-based solutions to make information management more effortless. However, over the last 20 years, the dimensions of digital information that businesses were storing started to reach significant levels. Any internal transaction, external exchange, or communications from consumers are generating data. Additionally, as the internet enables businesses to increase the volume of their interactions with external players, namely, consumers, the volume of data businesses may collect is dramatically becoming significant.

The new amount of information that businesses manage has widely been defined as one of the most significant outcomes of digital technology availability and one of the most relevant causes of digital transformation. First, businesses should develop processes to collect such data, make the information flow within the organization, and develop new strategies to transform (Sumbal et al., 2017).

Even SMEs are included in such a panorama. Indeed, SMEs currently have huge information quantities internally at their disposal concerning the past. Now, internal data constantly flow to managers from any machine and are assimilated into cloud databases. Likewise, most SMEs currently have at least a social media account and a website (Troise et al., 2022). Consumer interactions in such environments may generate data time by time. Accordingly, it is relevant even for SMEs to have diverse systems to *normalize* data in a standard format. This approach will allow organization-wide comprehension and the possibility of matching consumers' data with production data to optimize performance (Bousdekis et al., 2019).

Digitization of data then affects any relationship in SMEs' lives and can potentially increase competitiveness.

ii. *Disruption*

Integrating Industry 4.0 digital technologies into existing businesses is an example of disruptive innovation. Such technologies can influence any existing process within the company. For example, because of digital technologies, communication within the firm may change. First, digital communication is frequently faster and cheaper than traditional communication. Second, everyone involved in business life currently can potentially access common databases containing information, thus making the decision processes faster. Third, digital technologies are enablers of automation and new production processes. Finally, digital technologies allow businesses to be more in touch with consumers and to sell different offerings. Thus, they are also changing existing value-creating processes (Rialti, Caliandro et al., 2018).

At this moment, it emerges how digital technologies will disrupt the way most businesses are running their day-to-day operations. Consequently, to cope with potential disruptions, companies will have to transform by diffusing a 'digitally oriented culture' within themselves.

In such a regard, the investments that businesses will have to make toward reskilling the workforce are the first pivotal action that may be undertaken. Any change starts necessarily with many smaller steps; therefore, it is necessary to evaluate the status of the business and then select the champions of the change.

Disruption brought to the table by 4.0 technology is not simply the digitalization of the processes; it is mainly basing everything on data instead of commonly accepted practices. The ways of production, how processes are managed, and how consumer profiling is conducted will change abruptly at the end of the transformation (Aversa et al., 2021). As an example, paper documents and managerial tasks concerning pattern identifications will be replaced by data and AI, which will create upset and eventually 'rage against the machines', with people trying to override digital procedures.

For SMEs, ongoing 4.0 will cause even more excellent resistance. Most companies are managed through informal procedures, and knowledge is still not codified in most cases. In particular, it is then necessary to understand the principal technologies that will be included and then build the change on the primary desired outcomes.

iii. *Dematerialization*

Apart from being capable of digitalizing all the information a business may possess, digital technology diffusion also triggered so-called digital dematerialization. Digital technology functionalities are currently capable of replacing most of the functionalities of many traditional goods. For example, the camera roll industry was completely dematerialized by the emergence of digital cameras. Camera roll is no longer required to save photos aside for small communities of aficionados. Similarly, the music CD industry was completely obliterated first by the emergence of players such as Napster, which provided free music before becoming illegal, and iTunes, which allows people to download digital music on their phones. A more recent example is the printed books industry, which is being replaced by the diffusion of e-books.

While in the early stages of the digital revolution, the speed of dematerialization was not dramatic, in the current day, its rate is changing many industries in a dramatic fashion. Therefore, businesses have found themselves needing to react to these changes. While several historic companies went bankrupt, many successful stories exist (Kauffman & Wang, 2008). Precisely, businesses that could turn themselves into digital services or product providers succeeded amidst the turbulences caused by dematerialization. As an example, some newspapers were able to become primarily digital, thus avoiding getting bankrupt like the ones deciding to focus primarily on printed versions. Similarly, businesses that were able to adopt hybrid strategies survived. A relevant example of adopting a hybrid strategy is represented by music businesses that focused on selling physical goods such as MP3 players and digital music. Finally, another successful strategy to survive digital transformation is to refocus the company to become a supplier of IT firms, as in the case of camera producers that turned out to produce optical lenses for smartphone producers (www.inc.com).

There is no specific best way to survive. However, businesses capable of adapting by turning completely or partly digital will indeed have a competitive edge over those anchored to legacy business models.

SMEs then must consider how their data will be transformed into digital data. Initially, such a transformation will cause huge havoc within the business, as traditional archives will no longer exist in the conventional form. Digital cloud archives, empowered by blockchain protocols that may allow data traceability, hold the potential to create digital databases ensuring traceability and duplicability.

The possibility of having all the data digitally may allow us to unpack their potential more than ever. Through simple BDA tools, SMEs may obtain information about their processes and consumers, identifying potential cues that have not been observed before (Buhalis & Volchek, 2021). Hence, in SMEs, whether they can include data within their processes, they may change their business models and increase the reach of pursuit opportunities.

iv. *Demonetization*

In the digital era, money is being increasingly removed from the equations underlying the economic context. This is happening in two ways.

On the one hand, money is getting digital. New payment technologies embedded in personal devices, such as digital wallets, allow people to avoid the usage of notes. Digital wallets have dematerialized conventional wallet users (businesses and consumers) by enabling them to pay with their smartphones, tablets, and computers. These wallets are linked to real bank accounts, but they are helping a whole new ensemble of payment methods that are more secure and traceable than existing physical money (Ghosh et al., 2017).

On the other hand, money is becoming increasingly necessary to purchase several digital services. While it may seem counterintuitive, consumers may obtain a service for free in a digital environment by providing the provider with their own data. This occurs in two kinds of cases. First, final consumers may download apps or join an online platform by logging in with their information. Second, businesses may download free software in the exchange of information. Suppose we observe this phenomenon from a business-oriented perspective. In that case, it clearly explains the need for businesses to try to find a way to create value while giving away services of digital products for free. Accordingly, the best solution is to create value from consumer data by selling them or using them for marketing campaigns (Crain, 2018).

Demonetization initially did not have huge effects on SMEs. Most money transactions were still occurring regularly (i.e., cash for small amounts and traditional checks or other kinds of wire transfers for larger ones). The more B2C and B2B consumers started to adopt digital payments; the more transformation affected SMEs (Ardito et al., 2018). First, a mobile point of sales (POS) emerged, allowing even the transfer of smaller amounts of money. Then, in a second moment, mobile phones endowed with radio-frequency identification (RFID) allowed the possibility to pay through mobile apps directly in-store or in the factory. SMEs thus found themselves in need of updating their procedures. Digital payments allowed, in fact reach new consumers even when they do not have available cash. It made profiling and targeting easier, as payments through mobile apps allowed us to trace the individual user more accurately as more data flowed between the seller and the purchaser (De Luca et al., 2021). Likewise, it allowed better management of in- and out-cash flows and reduced risks related to cash-based economies. New typologies of money, such as digital currencies (i.e., cryptocurrencies), also allowed the use of innovative credit instruments and the sale of products in different environments (i.e., advanced online shops).

To reap these benefits, what emerged as fundamental was the implementation of tools to manage such economic flows (Thampanya et al., 2020). Aside from traditional POS, it was necessary to update registers and devices to maintain the business's accounting.

v. *Democratization*

Democratization in the internet research context describes how access to the web is becoming commonly available in most countries. While the world is still far from achieving worldwide democracy using the internet or in the use of the internet (i.e., many countries are still limiting internet access to many contents), internet connection is becoming ubiquitous as a consequence of the diffusion of high-speed cable-based broadband and mobile broadband in most countries. More than 3.5 billion people will have access to the Internet by 2025. In such a regard, most people may currently express their opinion on the web, thus becoming capable of influencing someone else. The diffusion of internet access also fosters human and machine connections. Therefore, employees and consumers may exchange data about service performance and device status.

Democratization is, therefore about the increasing availability of internet access points. As more people, businesses, and machines are connected to the Internet, the more data will be freely available, the more opportunity to obtain practical knowledge from the internet, and more insights will emerge.

Democratization may be observed regarding SMEs' impact from two perspectives: a positive one and a double-faced one. The first concerns the growing accessibility for SMEs in web environments. As the internet is democratic, even small businesses may create their own space and attract massive attention with respect to their products. The most common example pertains to the possibility of being present in many social media environments, and online stores create an ad hoc space (Krishen et al., 2021). The second perspective regards the fact that consumers may directly interact with businesses in a 'democratic' way. Consumers populating virtual spaces could in fact quickly diffuse their opinions (e-WOM) and ask companies for greater information. However, as these comments and contents are not necessarily positive, SMEs, as their larger counterparts, will need to develop procedures to manage consumers in such environments and to separate positive interactions from negative comments. Creating these systems and processes is fundamental, particularly in the current hater-dominated era, where people start tarnishing brands' reputations even for fun through fake news.

vi. *Disintermediation*

Among the most double-edged effects of internet diffusion, it is possible to find disintermediation. Disintermediation is related to the reduction in intermediaries between businesses and consumers caused by the distribution of digital applications such as e-commerce platforms or other platforms enabling users to skip an intermediary. Disintermediation is all about cutting out 'middlemen' or replacing them with digital ones (Andal-Ancion et al., 2003).

Hence, from a consumer's perspective, online platforms can reduce the costs of their purchases. The middleman percentage is disappearing from the final price. Likewise, consumers may currently confront prices online, looking at the most convenient solution. From a business perspective, instead, it is causing the need to rethink how to contact consumers. Businesses will need to develop websites capable of communicating their portfolio to consumers in place of intermediaries. Nevertheless, suppose the business itself was an intermediary. In that case, managers will need to think about how to turn into a digital intermediary and, thus how a transformation from physical to digital service will be required in this case.

Such a phenomenon in recent times has been defined as platform economy diffusion (or *platformization*). New digital channels have allowed the emergence of some specific intermediaries (platforms) that are replacing traditional intermediaries (Chen et al., 2021). Media presented to SMEs several additional opportunities concerning traditional mechanisms. First, they allow direct contact with potential consumers at lower costs (i.e., platforms may simply ask an access or a monthly fee in place of a percentage of sales). Second, they allow the promotion of more products than the ones that a sales agent may usually carry with them. Third, it dramatically extends the reach of SME marketing strategies. Platforms are not limited to a specific context; they potentially allow us to reach any consumers connected to the internet. Fourth, many platforms automatically organize the most convenient shipping method and manage to invoice automatically. Finally, they allow direct communication and feedback mechanisms from consumers, which may trigger others' purchases.

Platforms exist in either B2B or B2C form. A case concerning the first one may be represented by the Alibaba Business platform, which allows businesses to purchase and sell raw material and machinery online. In such an environment, suppliers and direct purchasers coexist and interact. Amazon and eBay are the most used B2BC databases (Krings et al., 2021).

While the platform economy presents several benefits for SMEs, managers should always be aware that direct personal relationships with consumers may disappear when using a platform. In such a regard, developing suitable and consumer-friendly feedback mechanisms to maintain a relationship with consumers will be relevant.

vii. *Decentralization*

Digital technologies are causing individuals to 'take in their hand' the control of several services. Traditionally, consumers select a service according to service providers' availability or purchase a product from nearby shops. In the digital era, they may connect and decide which service provider is the best and cheapest for them or decide which product to buy from an online platform.

This phenomenon is called decentralization. This is related to the fact that now a service provider or an e-tailer from another world may provide consumers with a service at home. For example, Deliveroo or Uber Eats enable consumers to obtain food at home from a restaurant far away. Similarly, using Amazon, a consumer may order a product from another country and receive it in a few days.

This aspect, which is related to *platformization*, also allows businesses to decentralize several of their internal nonfundamental operations. Crowds in the online environment may enable SMEs to recur to collective intelligence forms, which could help in decision-making processes. On the other hand, some platforms offer SMEs the opportunity to outsource tasks characterizing their traditional management, such as data analysis (De Luca et al., 2021).

2.3 Digitalization in Industry 4.0: A New Challenge and Opportunity for SME Marketers

Digital transformation is the profound transformation of business and organizational activities, processes, competencies, and models to fully leverage the changes and opportunities of a mix of digital technologies and their accelerating impact across society strategically and prioritized, with present and future shifts in mind.

The advent of digital technologies is causing significant changes (or disruption) to how businesses run their day-to-day operations and how they create value. While in the past, digital technologies mainly were used for tasks in very few specific value chains, digital technologies such as computers, sensors, and the internet are currently ubiquitous within any business. Such technologies are indeed embedded into most machines and are fundamental to making these machines work correctly. Additionally, digital technologies such as online platforms and websites have significantly affected the implementation of successful marketing strategies and the traditional offerings made by businesses. This is the 4.0 era, where technologies are substantially autonomous and ubiquitous. Nothing will look the same in ten years, and it is necessary to consider how it will change any business area (Pitsis et al., 2020).

In fact, in the current economic environment, more than 96% of businesses in most developed economies use digital technology for digital marketing or production processes (Palattella et al., 2016). Similarly, consumers' lives are also pervaded by digital technologies. Approximately 3 billion people access the internet for job-related tasks or amusement. Approximately 89% of millennials and 72% of baby boomers use at least one online platform daily (Berman, 2012).

As the use of any digital technology generates some data, data available to any business consequently reached levels that were not imaginable just a few years ago. These data principally come from two sources. On the one hand, internal data may come from operations; hence, businesses may now know the status of every process better than ever. On the other hand, they may come directly from consumers through online feedback. It is not surprising then that most of the private institutions dealing with business and industry reports, that is, Bain & Company, Accenture, BCG, or Gartner, are stressing how all these new available information businesses will change radically over the next decade (Kaplan & Haenlein, 2016).

Accordingly, digital disruption caused by the availability of new data and new digital technologies is having several macro effects on modern business. In detail, digital technologies (tied-up with the availability of new data) can cause (1) improved performance of business processes and activities, (2) the reduction of frontstage and backstage costs, (3) the emergence of new touchpoints between consumers and businesses, (4) increased involvement of customers in product or service development and the development of new offerings, and (5) better delivery of knowledge-intensive services (Demirkan et al., 2016). This vision is coherent with the basic assumption, presented in the first part of this paragraph, that digital technologies may cause significant disruptions to what concerns the production processes and day-to-day operations or products and services (Berman, 2012).

Regarding the impact of digital technologies on internal operations and activities, it has been widely observed that integrating computers and the Internet in traditional processes may save a considerable amount of money in modern businesses. For example, technologies based on the Internet of Things (IoT) can allow managers to monitor the performance of every machine or process at any moment. IoT in the business context is defined as a possible network of appliances and other items embedded with software, sensors, actuators, and internet connectivity, enabling these machines and things to connect to the internet and collect and exchange data. Because of all this, it shows disruptive potential (Wortmann & Flüchter, 2015). Because of the IoT, people in charge of a machine or a process can have a complete overview of how these machines or processes are performing in real time via suite software capable of transforming digital information into percentages of utilization, information about wasting of resources, and outputs.

Additionally, because the IoT allows machines to be connected to the internet and internal databases, the IoT also offers the possibility to collect and analyze such data. This possibility will enable managers or decision makers to build time series about trends in performance, to make comparisons with benchmarks, and to have an overview of the simultaneous implementation of the whole business (Caputo et al., 2016). Consequently, the IoT is also fundamental to identifying bottlenecks in processes.

Similarly, comparable digital technologies can prove instrumental for supply chain management. Some supply chain management or enterprise resource planning (ERP) software allows different organizations to dialog digitally constantly using the internet and shared databases. Thus, via these tools, a supplier may immediately know which quantity of a specific resource a business has just used, and subsequently, the supplier can resupply that item in a short time or without any additional communication. Two other technologies may help the work of these software:

RFID(radio-frequency identification) and barcodes. RFID technologies are based on tags attached to an item (in this case, a resource coming from a supplier) emitting a radio frequency communicating reading tool information about the item itself. Barcode-based technologies work similarly; the only inconvenience is that barcode readers need to be in the reader's line of sight (while in the case of RFID, the reader can also be some meter away from the item).

Despite the differences, such technologies may be integrated with software, thus allowing us to collect information about the products in a dataset and share information within the company and with suppliers. Managers and decision makers may therefore know the status of warehouses and order replenishment. As it is possible to observe, integrating information about production processes from sensors embedded into machines (IoT) and information about warehouses and required supplies may allow us to plan the production processes in extreme detail, utilize resources and increase efficiency (Liu et al., 2011). However, technologies such as these two may offer additional benefits to businesses if they are also embedded in computer systems with artificial intelligence (AI). AI is transforming machines into 'intelligent agents' that can perceive what is happening around them and autonomously decide which action is the best to maximize the possibilities of achieving a goal. Thus, when computers obtain all the information they require, they can decide how many raw materials or components the production process needs, how many items need to be produced (and consequently the usage percentage of each machine), and how to make that efficiently. In addition, due to the internet connection, computers may send input to devices and order them to take the right action in real time without needing someone to program them again (Ransbotham et al., 2017). As most computer decisions are frequently less biased (and more objective) than human decisions, using computers embedded with AI and connected to machines involved in a process may allow better exploitation of resources and increase productivity (Matt et al., 2015). Digital technologies can thus improve businesses' value chains; they can make them more efficient and effective. Consequently, most digital technologies are related to reduced internal costs due to lower waste of resources and improved production efficiency. However, these benefits will come at the expense of changing how a business runs its daily operations.

As previously assessed, digital technologies also play a huge role in concerns about changes occurring in traditional products, services, and marketing strategies. First, new digital platforms allow businesses to contact consumers using a personal digital tool at any moment. Social media or e-commerce platforms, for example, have created new touchpoints between companies and consumers (Kaplan & Haenlein, 2010). Businesses can now gather tons of information about how consumers perceive brands and products, their shopping behavior, and their social behavior. In addition, as these platforms are bidirectional, they also allow businesses to better communicate with consumers via online messages. How businesses engage consumers is totally different; now, companies may engage consumers in digital conversations capable of influencing their purchase behavior (Rialti et al., 2017). Hence, relationship management (CRM) is becoming digital, and businesses are investing their money in hiring specialists in communicate with consumers (Trainor et al., 2014). Second, due to the possibility of collecting and analyzing information from consumers with the help of digital technologies, businesses are implementing different processes to identify new offerings.

On the one hand, businesses develop or improve products using insights from consumers directly. Consumers' requests are now reaching businesses without any interference, as consumers may contact companies directly online. This is coherent with 'cocreation' theories, which imply that cocreation in a digital context occurs when consumers contribute to shaping a product or an offering with their digital feedback (Rialti, Caliandro et al., 2018). On the other hand, businesses may offer consumers additional services thanks to online channels. For example, if we consider e-tailers, it is possible to observe how any e-tailer may provide consumers with additional services by exploiting an e-commerce platform. Currently, most e-tailers can sell consumers additional services such as insurance or express expedition services, which may dramatically increase e-tailers' revenues. Similarly, by using online platforms, consumers may customize the products they are about to order (different colors, different packaging, etc.; Akter & Wamba, 2016). Digital technologies such as online platforms are fundamental to increasing digital business revenue streams (Berman, 2012). Third, digital technologies allow producers to enhance or augment existing products or services by integrating them into their digital technologies. Everyday objects are transforming. This is the case for products such as the ill-fated Google Glasses, which were glasses relying on an optical head-mounted display capable of giving information to the user.

Similarly, music has changed, as it is currently almost a complete digital product; in fact, the main way for most people to 'use' music is by downloading a song and listening to it using a digital artifact such as the iPhone. Fourth, digital technologies represent a new way for service providers to deliver services. For example, massive online open courses (MOOCs) are replacing many education-related services that universities previously delivered of educational institutes. Everyone can create an account and attend classes for free while sitting on their own sofa in their spare time (Hood et al., 2015; Kaplan & Haenlein, 2016). Finally, opportunities deriving from digital technologies are also changing how the salesforce relates to consumers. Via instruments such as tablets, the salesforce can now collect more consumer data or provide consumers with more information about a product (Westerman et al., 2014a).

Digital technologies may dramatically affect modern businesses. They may allow enterprises to simultaneously reduce costs and increase revenues. Moreover, according to the degree to which digital technologies affect the business, digital technologies may foster the emergence of entirely new business models. As an example, digital technologies may revolutionize how a business sells its products by using digital channels, thus cutting the intermediaries (Andal-Ancion et al., 2003). Similarly, a whole new business model is required when a business replaces physical products with digital ones (such as in the music industry case).

However, to manage the changes caused by digital technologies and data, modern businesses must invest properly in new procedures, processes, and systems to exploit the opportunities of the digital era. In the case of SMEs, such an evolutionary process may prove highly complex and challenging, even more than in any other typology of business. The size of SMEs puts them frequently at risk when the moment to underpin significant investment comes. Additionally, these businesses are frequently characterized by concentrated in one or few persons, which may be resistant to new technologies. Employees likewise may pose a challenge in I4.0 projects, as they are missing technological skills. Such elements may represent unsurpassable barriers to the change of the business.

Appropriately, studies on the impact of digital technologies on businesses have pointed out how businesses must change and completely *transform* to manage the change brought by digital technologies appropriately (Matt et al., 2015). In detail, digital transformation has been defined as the profound adaptation of business activities, processes, and competencies to fully leverage the changes and opportunities brought by digital technologies in a purposeful way (Demirkan et al., 2016). Therefore, the essence of this kind of business transformation consists of integrating digital technologies in business processes and routines, developing proper human resource digital skills, and managing outcomes of digitalization (Liu et al., 2011).

It is worth noting that not all businesses are required to transform in the same way digitally. Some micro businesses operating in sectors with low competition, for instance, may not require advanced digital technologies; in their case, maybe they do not need to disrupt a market, as they may not obtain any significant competitive advantage. The adoption of some essential technologies, such as mobile payment tools, may be sufficient to increase their market share. Likewise, basic ERP may improve inventory management, but it may not require AI. Similarly, businesses operating with huge margins may not need to transform in a short time digitally. They probably have very standardized routines generating economies of scale, and digital technologies may cause their margin to decrease due to the disruption to the traditional way of doing business (Andriole, 2010). Nevertheless, suppose a company is operating in a very competitive environment and competitors have already started to digitally transform, even with extremely high margins. In that case, the only way to remain competitive in the long run is to change too.

Moving from these premises, some questions still need to be answered:

- *What are the specific drivers of digital transformation?*
- *What is the essence of the digital transformation process?*
- *How can current businesses manage a digital transformation?*

Digital transformation, in detail, is a kind of technology-enabled transformation (Zhu et al., 2006).

As with most the transformation of this kind, on the one hand, digital transformation derives from four innovation-related characteristics, such as the relative advantages offered by (1) technological innovation, (2) the degree of compatibility between the innovative technology and the existing processes occurring within businesses, (3) the costs related to technology adoption, and (4) security and privacy concerns.

On the other hand, digital transformation is driven by four contextual factors, namely, (1) technological competence, (2) the size of the business, (3) the pressure that competitors are putting on the business, and (4) partner readiness (Oliveira & Martins, 2011).

It then emerges how digital transformation success is associated with innovation adoption and organizational behavior literatures. Consequently, first, the need for a digital transformation can be interpreted considering the diffusion of innovation theory (DOI), which postulates that the more an innovation starts to affect a business, the greater the company will try to integrate it (Nambisan et al., 2017). Second, according to the organizational behavior view, digital transformation may be explained using the technology-organization-environment (TOE) framework, which explains digital transformation as the corporate response to technological evolution and environmental turbulence (Chiu et al., 2017).

SMEs may then decide to digitally transform in an I4.0 fashion to reap the possible operational and marketing advantages deriving from technologies, particularly whether these benefits outweigh the economic costs and complexity related to implementation (Pitsis et al., 2020). Among the other principal theories explaining digital transformation in SMEs, research has frequently used technology acceptance models such as TAM and TAM2 (Krishen et al., 2021). It was observed that the perceived usefulness and ease of use of some mass-available technologies influenced the final actual use and performance of these tools in SMEs (Bigerna et al., 2021). Then, regarding the micro-level mechanisms that foster SMEs' adoption of I4.0 tools in marketing, dynamic capabilities represented a relevant theoretical approach to unpack the phenomenon. Dynamic capabilities are, in fact, organization-wide capabilities spurring disseminated practices capable of fostering the identification of new tools or the reconfiguration of existing information to exploit innovative opportunities.

Due to the several heterogeneous factors that may trigger the decision to digitally transform the business, any manager needs to conduct a series of evaluations and develop a strategic plan before starting a digital transformation process. In particular, before starting a digital transformation, managers need to evaluate (a) why they are considering the possibility of digital transformation and what may be the use/scope of digital technologies within the business, (b) what the challenges related to the integration of digital technologies, (c) what changes will the integration of digital technologies bring to existing product and processes and what will be the economic effect of such technologies (i.e., in terms of costs and benefits) and, simultaneously, (d) which actions are required to make the digital transformation faster and smoother.

Accordingly, managers need to identify the motivations underlying digital transformation in the first step. During this phase, managers must then distinguish whether they are pursuing the digital transformation for their own sake and self-accomplishment—that is, just to put on their resumes that they could manage a digital transformation or of obtaining some kind of economic benefit—or if the quest for greater integration of digital technologies into the business is motivated by some objective reasons.

Before starting the digital transformation endeavor, questions such as 'Is the digital transformation required to improve the way the business is producing something?', 'Is the digital transformation necessary to improve processes and remain competitive?', or 'Is the digital transformation coherent with what our competitors are going to do?' must be addressed by owners and managers (Westerman et al., 2012). The scope of the proposed digital transformation must be outlined and supported by evidence. As hinted through this chapter, usually, the main content of a digital transformation may be either the improvement of products, services, and marketing strategies (thus, the scope of the change is to improve sales or relationships with consumers), the integration of digital technologies into existing processes (to increase businesses' efficiency) or mixed (digitally reshaping offerings and products and developing a new business model) (Liu et al., 2011). According to the selected scope, during this preliminary evaluation of the motivations underlying the digital transformation, managers should also review existing digital technologies capable of addressing the prefixed scope and which ones are genuinely implementable in the business (Westerman & Bonnet, 2015). What a selected digital technology can and cannot do should be categorized to make the right choice. It is pointless to implement a system capable of scraping data from the web and analyzing these data if the only scope of the digital transformation is to manage the supply chain better.

Analyzing the challenges linked to integrating digital technologies into traditional processes is the second phase characterizing any digital transformation endeavor. To proceed, managers should first evaluate whether it will be possible to exploit at least some existing resources or assets (Majchrzak et al., 2016). The critical action that managers need to undertake is the evaluation of the possible fit between existing resources and competencies and the applied capabilities of the new digital technologies that will be adopted. Most of the existing machines, for example, can be enhanced by adding sensors to monitor production flow. Still, if the scope of digital transformation is to improve marketing reach, the addition of sensors to the machine may be worthless. Hence, managers should not limit the potential possibilities deriving from digital transformation, and evaluating the possibility of integrating new technologies into existing resources (or processes) is fundamental. It is absolute, as this evaluation determines the requirements for new tools (Westerman et al., 2012; Westerman & Bonnet, 2015). This is just the first challenge that managers must consider. Undeniably, managers should also assess the degree of digital skills currently possessed by the workforce. As stressed by most of the literature, employee resistance may prevent the successful realization of most digital transformations. It is straightforward to understand why employees matter in this equation. Employees are indeed the ones that will operate most of the new digital technologies and should monitor the correct execution of a process (Brynjolfsson & Hitt, 2000). Thus, if employees oppose using digital technologies, managers should invest in policies to convince them about the potential of such new instruments (Fitzgerald et al., 2014). After assessing the main technical and human resource-related challenges, managers may start to estimate the genuine efforts of implementing digital technologies.

After that, it will be relevant to evaluate which effects could be achieved by implementing a new technology despite possible difficulties. The main results of digital transformation depend on the identified scope and the kind of digital technology that will be implemented. This notwithstanding, the most common effects of digital transformation are related to increased efficiency in supply chain management, a smaller quantity of goods in inventories, more efficient production processes, faster knowledge flows between different business units, more information about consumers or their preferences, and improved CRM strategies (Brynjolfsson & Hitt, 2000). Indeed, building on Demirkan et al. (2016), these are the most common effects of technologies capable of gathering additional intelligence from internal processes or markets and, additionally, capable of quickly transferring such information to managers (thanks to internet speed). Based on the effects produced by digital transformation, managers may ultimately evaluate whether digital transformation will generate more costs or benefits (Vendrell-Herrero et al., 2017). Generally, if the digital transformation has been capable of achieving the expected results, it is possible to assume that it was successful. However, managers should consider several other elements to assess whether the digital transformation was successful. First, they can consider if the costs to complete the digital transformation surpassed the savings from more efficient management of the internal processes or operations. Second, they can consider the difference (if any) between the implementation costs and additional revenues from additional sales using a digital channel. Third, managers could consider the digital transformation substantially successful if the digital transformation costs did not overrun the costs predicted in the budget. Finally, they can evaluate the degree of success of digital transformation by considering the distance between effective and expected outcomes (Matt et al., 2015).

Notwithstanding any possible strategic plan developed by managers, no digital transformation can be successful if managers have not contemplated how to make this transformation easier. Several organization-related factors, such as a negative attitude from the workforce, attachment to legacy procedures or information systems, or generic resistance to innovation, may convince everyone involved about the possibility of stopping the digital transformation process. A digital transformation is a form of change affecting every kind of process and internal relationship; thus, managers should prepare the whole organization (and everyone involved in any method) for what will happen. This phenomenon should necessarily occur to pave the road for change. While a 'one size fits all' approach to digital transformation does not exist, pertinent literature has stressed several possibilities for making digital transformation easier. First, managers leading digital transformation should make the case for digital transformation. For example, they should explain to everyone how current technologies the business uses are outdated and, therefore, do not allow the business to be competitive anymore (Fitzgerald et al., 2014). Second, whenever the decision to consider digital transformation has been made, managers should set up a model to jointly evaluate the change based on an inclusive, participatory process (Hansen et al., 2011). To allow valuable data exchange, managers should include people skilled in the topic, such as informatic engineers and consultants, and people working in one of the areas that will be affected by the transformation.

Additionally, experts on digital technologies may explain the need to transform digitally more properly than managers. Coherently, managers should set up a series of meetings with employees to assess the importance of new digital technologies, analyze the pros and cons together, and debate their implementation before acting. The message that needs to be transmitted during employee meetings is that digital technologies are not replacing humans, but they may help everyone in their work (Liu et al., 2011). Third, managers should consequently focus on building up the digital transformation of existing skills and processes. This will make the change more accessible, allowing the exploitation of existing skills and resources (Fitzgerald et al., 2014). Fourth, before the digital transformation, managers should also remember to invest in training programs to improve workforce digital skills. Comprehension of innovation is fundamental to fostering everyone's innovation adoption. Therefore, managers should plan programs to endow everyone with skills such as statistics, computer programming, data analytics, digital process management, and digital marketing (www.futurelean.com). Economic and career incentives may play a role in motivating attendance to such programs. Reward plans are then fundamental to making 'champions' of the digital transformation process arising from the crowd.

Therefore, digital transformation managers should stimulate the emergence of a shared path toward transformation. This will enable the start of the change and make the transformative process more accessible, smoother, and faster. Indeed, the conversion will proceed only if managers can evaluate the technologies or their effects while creating a shared vision.

They are assessing the current level of preparation of the business facing digital transformation. Maturity models could provide relevant information to managers and consultants approaching such problems. Research on I4.0-related change identified I4.0 maturity assessment models employable in the SME context. Some traditional models, such as 'Reifsgradmodel Industrie 4.0' and 'Industry 4.0 Maturity Index', are not tailored for SMEs. However, the 'IMPULS Industrie 4.0 Readiness 2015' model may represent a temporary solution to this problem, as it includes the 'Outsiders' and 'Beginners' levels (which may consist of most SMEs) and may allow these businesses to identify the principal transformation objectives. A model capable of suitably detecting the distance between SMEs' status and I4.0 has yet to be developed.

Tools such as the IMPULS models could drive SMEs to shape the initial vision targeting I4.0, notably by assessing their status and developing maps concerning which processes must be transformed first. A clear plan is fundamental to challenging the technological revolution, and SMEs trying to digitalize without following a path have historically failed in such endeavors.

Only if a proper digital transformation strategy is being developed may a business be categorized in the future among the 'digirati' businesses, which are the digital-intensive businesses capable of exploiting digital innovation to create value (Westerman et al., 2012).

References

Akter, S., & Wamba, S. F. (2016). Big data analytics in E-commerce: A systematic review and agenda for future research. *Electronic Markets, 26*(2), 173–194.

Andal-Ancion, A., Cartwright, P. A., & Yip, G. S. (2003). The digital transformation of traditional businesses. *MIT Sloan Management Review, 44*(4), 34–42.

Andriole, S. J. (2010). Business impact of Web 2.0 technologies. *Communications of the ACM, 53*(12), 67–79.

Ardito, L., Petruzzelli, A. M., Panniello, U., & Garavelli, A. C. (2018). Towards Industry 4.0: Mapping digital technologies for supply chain management-marketing integration. *Business Process Management Journal, 25*(2), 323–346.

Aversa, J., Hernandez, T., & Doherty, S. (2021). Incorporating big data within retail organizations: A case study approach. *Journal of Retailing and Consumer Services, 60*, 102447.

Bagnoli, C., Dal Mas, F., & Massaro, M. (2019). The 4th industrial revolution: Business models and evidence from the field. *International Journal of E-Services and Mobile Applications (IJESMA), 11*(3), 34–47.

Berman, S. J. (2012). Digital transformation: Opportunities to create new business models. *Strategy & Leadership, 40*(2), 16–24.

Bigerna, S., Micheli, S., & Polinori, P. (2021). New generation acceptability towards durability and repairability of products: Circular economy in the era of the 4th industrial revolution. *Technological Forecasting and Social Change, 165*, 120558.

Bousdekis, A., Apostolou, D., & Mentzas, G. (2019). Predictive maintenance in the 4th industrial revolution: Benefits, business opportunities, and managerial implications. *IEEE Engineering Management Review, 48*(1), 57–62.

Brynjolfsson, E., & Hitt, L. M. (2000). Beyond computation: Information technology, organizational transformation and business performance. *Journal of Economic Perspectives, 14*(4), 23–48.

Buhalis, D., & Volchek, K. (2021). Bridging marketing theory and big data analytics: The taxonomy of marketing attribution. *International Journal of Information Management, 56*, 102253.

Caputo, A., Marzi, G., & Pellegrini, M. M. (2016). The internet of things in manufacturing innovation processes: Development and application of a conceptual framework. *Business Process Management Journal, 22*(2), 383–402.

Chen, H., Chiang, R. H., & Storey, V. C. (2012). Business intelligence and analytics: From big data to big impact. *MIS Quarterly, 36*(4), 1165–1188.

Chen, Y., Richter, J. I., & Patel, P. C. (2021). Decentralized governance of digital platforms. *Journal of Management, 47*(5), 1305–1337.

Chiu, C. Y., Chen, S., & Chen, C. L. (2017). An integrated perspective of TOE framework and innovation diffusion in broadband mobile applications adoption by enterprises. *International Journal of Management, Economics and Social Sciences (IJMESS), 6*(1), 14–39.

Crain, M. (2018). The limits of transparency: Data brokers and commodification. *New Media & Society, 20*(1), 88–104.

Dash, G., Kiefer, K., & Paul, J. (2021). Marketing-to-millennials: Marketing 4.0, customer satisfaction and purchase intention. *Journal of Business Research, 122*, 608–620.

De Luca, L. M., Herhausen, D., Troilo, G., & Rossi, A. (2021). How and when do big data investments pay off? The role of marketing affordances and service innovation. *Journal of the Academy of Marketing Science, 49*(4), 790–810.

Demirkan, H., Spohrer, J. C., & Welser, J. J. (2016). Digital innovation and strategic transformation. *IT Professional, 18*(6), 14–18.

Dickson, P. R. (2000). Understanding the trade winds: The global evolution of production, consumption, and the Internet. *Journal of Consumer Research, 27*(1), 115–122.

Fitzgerald, M., Kruschwitz, N., Bonnet, D., & Welch, M. (2014). Embracing digital technology: A new strategic imperative. *MIT Sloan Management Review, 55*(2), 1–8.

Gandomi, A., & Haider, M. (2015). Beyond the hype: Big data concepts, methods, and analytics. *International Journal of Information Management, 35*(2), 137–144.

Gbosbal, S., & Kim, S. K. (1986). Building effective intelligence systems for competitive advantage. *Sloan Management Review, 28*(1), 49–71.

Ghosh, S., Majumder, A., Goswami, J., Kumar, A., Mohanty, S. P., & Bhattacharyya, B. K. (2017). Swing-pay: One card meets all user payment and identity needs: A digital card module using NFC and biometric authentication for peer-to-peer payment. *IEEE Consumer Electronics Magazine, 6*(1), 82–93.

Hansen, A. M., Kraemmergaard, P., & Mathiassen, L. (2011). Rapid adaptation in digital transformation: A participatory process for engaging IS and business leaders. *MIS Quarterly Executive, 10*(4), 5.

Hood, N., Littlejohn, A., & Milligan, C. (2015). Context counts: How learners' contexts influence learning in a MOOC. *Computers & Education, 91*, 83–91.

Kaplan, A. M., & Haenlein, M. (2010). Users of the world, unite! The challenges and opportunities of social media. *Business Horizons, 53*(1), 59–68.

Kaplan, A. M., & Haenlein, M. (2016). Higher education and the digital revolution: About MOOCs, SPOCs, social media, and the Cookie Monster. *Business Horizons, 59*(4), 441–450.

Kauffman, R. J., & Wang, B. (2008). Tuning into the digital channel: Evaluating business model characteristics for Internet firm survival. *Information Technology and Management, 9*(3), 215–232.

Kim, J. (2018). Are countries ready for the new meso revolution? Testing the waters for new industrial change in Korea. *Technological Forecasting and Social Change, 132*, 34–39.

Krings, W., Palmer, R., & Inversini, A. (2021). Industrial marketing management digital media optimization for B2B marketing. *Industrial Marketing Management, 93*, 174–186.
Krishen, A. S., Dwivedi, Y. K., Bindu, N., & Kumar, K. S. (2021). A broad overview of interactive digital marketing: A bibliometric network analysis. *Journal of Business Research, 131*, 183–195.
Liu, D. Y.; Chen, S. W., & Chou, T. C. (2011). Resource fit in digital transformation: Lessons learned from the CBC Bank global e-banking project. *Management Decision, 49*(10), 1728–1742.
Ljungqvist, A., & Wilhelm, W. J. (2003). IPO pricing in the dot-com bubble. *The Journal of Finance, 58*(2), 723–752.
Loebbecke, C., & Picot, A. (2015). Reflections on societal and business model transformation arising from digitization and big data analytics: A research agenda. *The Journal of Strategic Information Systems, 24*(3), 149–157.
Majchrzak, A., Markus, M. L., & Wareham, J. (2016). Designing for digital transformation: Lessons for information systems research from the study of ICT and societal challenges. *MIS Quarterly, 40*(2), 267–277.
Matt, C., Hess, T., & Benlian, A. (2015). Digital transformation strategies. *Business & Information Systems Engineering, 57*(5), 339–343.
Mowery, D. C., & Simcoe, T. (2002). Is the internet a US invention?—an economic and technological history of computer networking. *Research Policy, 31*(8-9), 1369–1387.
Nambisan, S., Lyytinen, K., Majchrzak, A., & Song, M. (2017). Digital innovation management: Reinventing innovation management research in a digital world. *MIS Quarterly, 41*(1), 223–238.
Oliveira, T., & Martins, M. F. (2011). Literature review of information technology adoption models at firm level. *Electronic Journal of Information Systems Evaluation, 14*(1), 110.
Palattella, M. R., Dohler, M., Grieco, A., Rizzo, G., Torsner, J., Engel, T., & Ladid, L. (2016). Internet of things in the 5G era: Enablers, architecture, and business models. *IEEE Journal on Selected Areas in Communications, 34*(3), 510–527.
Peppard, J. (2000). Customer relationship management (CRM) in financial services. *European Management Journal, 18*(3), 312–327.
Pitsis, T. S., Beckman, S. L., Steinert, M., Oviedo, L., & Maisch, B. (2020). Designing the future: Strategy, design, and the 4th industrial revolution—an introduction to the special issue. *California Management Review, 62*(2), 5–11.

Ransbotham, S., Kiron, D., Gerbert, P., & Reeves, M. (2017). Reshaping business with artificial intelligence: Closing the gap between ambition and action. *MIT Sloan Management Review, 59*(1).

Rialti, R., Caliandro, A., Zollo, L., & Ciappei, C. (2018). Co-creation experiences in social media brand communities: Analyzing the main types of co-created experiences. *Spanish Journal of Marketing-ESIC, 22*(2), 122–141.

Rialti, R., Zollo, L., Pellegrini, M. M., & Ciappei, C. (2017). Exploring the antecedents of brand loyalty and electronic word of mouth in social-media-based brand communities: Do gender differences matter? *Journal of Global Marketing, 30*(3), 147–160.

Sumbal, M. S., Tsui, E., & See-to, E. W. (2017). Interrelationship between big data and knowledge management: An exploratory study in the oil and gas sector. *Journal of Knowledge Management, 21*(1), 180–196.

Thampanya, N., Nasir, M. A., & Huynh, T. L. D. (2020). Asymmetric correlation and hedging effectiveness of gold & cryptocurrencies: From pre-industrial to the 4th industrial revolution. *Technological Forecasting and Social Change, 159*, 120195.

Trainor, K. J., Andzulis, J. M., Rapp, A., & Agnihotri, R. (2014). Social media technology usage and customer relationship performance: A capabilities-based examination of social CRM. *Journal of Business Research, 67*(6), 1201–1208.

Trento, S., Bannò, M., & D'Allura, G. M. (2018). The impact of the 4th industrial revolution on the high-tech industry. *Symphonya. Emerging Issues in Management, 2*, 145–157.

Troise, C., Corvello, V., Ghobadian, A., & O'Regan, N. (2022). How can SMEs successfully navigate VUCA environment: The role of agility in the digital transformation era. *Technological Forecasting and Social Change, 174*, 121227.

Vendrell-Herrero, F., Bustinza, O. F., Parry, G., & Georgantzis, N. (2017). Servitization, digitization and supply chain interdependency. *Industrial Marketing Management, 60*, 69–81.

Westerman, G., & Bonnet, D. (2015). Revamping your business through digital transformation. *MIT Sloan Management Review, 56*(3), 10.

Westerman, G., Tannou, M., Bonnet, D., Ferraris, P., & McAfee, A. (2012). The digital advantage: How digital leaders outperform their peers in every industry. *MIT Sloan Management and Capgemini Consulting, 2*, 2–23.

Westerman, G., Bonnet, D., & McAfee, A. (2014a). *Leading digital: Turning technology into business transformation*. Harvard Business Press.

Wortmann, F., & Flüchter, K. (2015). Internet of things. *Business & Information Systems Engineering, 57*(3), 221–224.

Xu, L., He, W., & Li, S. (2014). Internet of things in industries: A survey. *IEEE Transactions on Industrial Informatics, 10*(4), 2233–2243.

Zhu, K., Dong, S., Xu, S. X., & Kraemer, K. L. (2006). Innovation diffusion in global contexts: Determinants of post-adoption digital transformation of European companies. *European Journal of Information Systems, 15*(6), 601–616.

Zollo, L., Rialti, R., Marrucci, A., & Ciappei, C. (2022). How do museums foster loyalty in tech-savvy visitors? The role of social media and digital experience. *Current Issues in Tourism, 25*(18), 2991–3008.

3

New Technologies and SMEs' Business Model: 'Marketization 4.0'

3.1 The Key Drivers Shaping Future Digital Trends

As assessed through the previous paragraphs, companies' need to digitally transform is not spontaneous; it depends on the degree of diffusion of digital technologies in the environment surrounding the business (Chiu et al., 2017). Companies, in effect, may not truly need to transform, but if competitors and customers are changing, they will need too to adapt to the new environment. However, any business that is stopping innovating for too long is at risk of losing competitiveness with respect to other players. The integration of computers, the internet, and automation in production processes may give a competitor a competitive edge over his or her own business (i.e., shorter delivery times, lower production costs, or increased revenue margins). Hence, if managers want the business to be outperformed by competitors, they need to start the digital transformation process.

Similarly, because of consumers' new consumption habits, a business will have to transform too. For instance, if most consumers purchase more products online than offline, the business will need to develop

R. Rialti, L. Zollo, *Digital Transformation of SME Marketing Strategies*,
https://doi.org/10.1007/978-3-031-33646-1_3

e-commerce platforms to avoid being forgotten by consumers (Westerman et al., 2012). How a company will transform and why it will transform is related to production technologies and marketing technologies' digital trends.

Building on an operation- and production-based perspective, the two most recent digital trends concerning internal operations and perspectives are related to the Internet of Things (IoT) and Industry 4.0. On the one hand, according to research on the IoT, the future of production processes is linked to the future capability of machines to adjust production volumes autonomously and to detect mistakes in a production process. On the other hand, according to Industry 4.0 research, the future of the business will pass through the possibility of developing a 'distributed production environment' or of benefiting from opportunities to exploit 'cloud-based manufacturing' or 'distributed manufacturing'. In terms of distributed environments, they have been defined as business environments populated by a mixture of physical and digital items that perform integrated tasks regardless of physical location (Kehoe & Boughton, 2001). The cloud-based manufacturing, instead, has been defined as a networked manufacturing model that exploits on-demand access to a collection of shared distributed manufacturing resources that can be assembled to form a temporary production line (Caputo et al., 2016). It will not be unusual in the future to have businesses with productive plants managed from remote positions thanks to internet connections. In some cases, even we will assist in the birth of some sort of nonexistent business dealing only with design and outsourcing every production phase to a shared production center.

Nevertheless, as previously stressed, digital trends in operations and production are not the only trends a business should be worried about, and new digital technologies that may be used by consumers will matter as well. Consumers' purchasing habits have dramatically changed, thanks to ubiquitous internet access via smartphones, tablets, and laptops. Indeed, consumers may now decide to purchase something at any moment of the day while performing another task. While most B2C businesses have already implemented e-commerce, the following challenges they will have to face will be how to maximize sales in the current environment. To do so, new customized advertising and promotions based on insights from consumers' analytics, virtual reality, new payment methods allowing consumers to make payments easier, and new CRM strategies will become less critical every day.

New trends that may affect consumers' habits will significantly impact SMEs too and will impact them very soon.

Consistently, it was thoroughly assessed that through I4.0 technologies, the way SMEs built their marketing strategies might change abruptly. First, it is possible to observe how pure I4.0 technologies such as 3D printing, may allow the development of completely innovative products in a shorter time and promote extreme customization for consumers. Second, although IoT, it is possible to collect more data than ever from consumers during their interactions in the store (De Luca et al., 2021). Then, it is possible to assume that BDA and AI businesses may attempt to forecast consumer behavior over time and create better CRM strategies. The more consumers feel the business is close to them, the more willing they are to purchase its products.

It is all a matter of selecting the right technology for the right purpose. Therefore, how the specific technology may influence how businesses operate and SME marketing strategies will be observed.

3.2 A Holistic and Integrated Overview of New Technology Implementation in SMEs

As for any other generic company, new digital trends are currently revolutionizing SMEs' way of doing business as well. New technologies may make process control and improvement easier or improve consumers' experiences. In fact, as previously assessed, digital technologies may help managers streamline their internal operations. However, digital technologies (including those used mainly by consumers) will also change the way SMEs deal with consumers. Consumers' adoption of digital technologies has been identified as one of the principal causes of the decrease in traditional SMEs' revenues. This is particularly true if we consider that every day, an increasing number of consumers renounce purchasing products in a physical store and opt to use virtual stores. This specific phenomenon started in the early 2000s with the emergence of e-commerce platforms, yet it is still occurring, and every year, electronic retailers (e-tailers) such as Amazon or Yoox erode the market shares of traditional retailers (Delone & McLean, 2004). The push from consumers at different levels is the main factor influencing the paths businesses choose. This is particularly true in the case of SMEs, which rely on constant selling to continue to generate cash flows. Following consumer preferences was not only a matter of adaptation concerning change but also a matter of survival. The same could be said due to competitive push. The more SMEs' larger counterparts started to adopt solutions that bypassed physical selling, the more SMEs needed adaptation.

Traditional SMEs hence have found themselves in a turbulent environment requiring them to react, as most of the principal different and complementary players started to digitally transform to survive. The very first competitive response from traditional players was to develop e-commerce platforms, too, thus beginning to compete with e-tailers on their home turf. However, e-tailers, at least in the beginning, proved to be too complicated an opponent to be defeated simply with in-house e-commerce platforms. Hence, new mixed models (i.e., the use of digital technologies to improve the efficiency or in-store experience) emerged as a possible solution to compete with 100% digital players. Accordingly, several digital technologies have emerged as fundamental for current SMEs to be competitive. Namely, some of these technologies are smart beacons and RFID, IoT, virtual and augmented reality, mobile and digital payment options, artificial intelligence, and blockchain. While all seven technologies will undoubtedly impact both processes and consumers' behavior, the first two of these will principally impact SMEs' efficiency. The third and the fourth will mostly impact consumers' experience. The fifth will enable SMEs to process more data while dealing with consumers. The sixth will instead allow SMEs to trace all their online transactions while ensuring more privacy to consumers.

In detail, technologies that affect SMEs in the 4.0 era are the following listed technologies, which can be divided into basic and supportive technologies. The first category includes sensors and actuators, smart beacons (such as RFID and RTLS), mobile technology, and cybersecurity tools.

The supportive ones, instead, include communication and networking (IoT), embedded systems (cyber-physical infrastructure) and cloud systems, additive manufacturing, adaptive robotics, virtualization technologies (Virtual Reality [VR] and augmented reality [AR]), and simulations, data analytics and artificial intelligence, mobile payment methods and tools (Ustundag & Cevikcan, 2017).

As the classification suggests, basic technologies enable the whole technological architecture to work as expected. SMEs should then invest in the initial phase in the selection of the right ones among these tools to make the entire system function as expected. The second ones instead are ancillary and should be selected according to the specific need of the business and the specific objective that is going to be pursued in the transformation. This second group of technologies thereby allows for the perfection of marketing strategies by increasing the data accuracy and subsequently the service level that could be offered to businesses.

3.2.1 Sensors and Actuators

Sensors are devices that transform a physical parameter into an electrical impulse. Actuators are devices that convert an electrical signal into a physical action. Sensors and actuators are the basic technology for any embedded system. Typically, one or more microcontrollers (control units) monitor the sensors and actuators needed to interact with the real world. The sensors handle the signal processing, and the actuators autonomously monitor the environmental state, correcting it if necessary.

The most common application in the context of Industry 4.0 for SMEs concerns systems that make it possible to monitor product quality in the supply chain (i.e., the packaging is equipped with integrated sensors connected to a cloud system). Such systems may continuously record data relevant to product quality, such as temperature, shock, or humidity.

The main advantages are as follows:

1. Real-time tracking along the entire production or service system
2. Continuous documentation and data collection to support big data analytics
3. Deep learning and knowledge extraction

3.2.2 Smart Beacons and Radio Frequency Identification (RFID)

Smart beacons and radio frequency identification tags were among the first digital technologies adopted by SMEs.

Smart beacons have been defined as 'a small Bluetooth radio transmitter. It's kind of like a lighthouse, as it repeatedly transmits a single signal that other devices can see. Instead of emitting a visible light, it broadcasts a radio signal made up of a combination of letters and numbers transmitted on a regular interval of approximately 1/10th of a second. A Bluetooth-equipped device like a smartphone can "see" a beacon once it is in range, much like sailors looking for a lighthouse to know where they are' (www.kontact.io). RFID tags are technological tools capable of transmitting a radio frequency signal to an RFID reader capable of transforming that signal into text information about the product (Caputo et al., 2016). RFID may be either active or passive. Active ones transmit the signal constantly. Passive neurons transmit a signal only when activated by an active input from a reader. RFID may only signal basic information and the distance from the object's reader. Real-Time Locating Systems (RTLS), instead, constantly transmit a GPS signal enabling the possibility of receiving the exact positioning of the object.

As it is possible to understand from their characteristics, such technologies' main uses are related to the possibility of monitoring the position of consumers and products within a specific area. Specifically, smart beacon-implanted devices such as smartphones can help businesses track the usual paths of a person within a store and then know their usual shopping habits. Henceforth, businesses can change the locations of products usually purchased by the same category of consumers to make it easier for them to find what they are looking for. In addition, whether such devices have display or some way to communicate with consumers, they will allow businesses to provide consumers with shopping suggestions or messages about personalized sales promotions (Fulgoni, 2014). As such, smart beacons are fundamental to delivering consumers with stimuli to give them incentives to purchase more products. This is particularly true considering that many personal devices currently have beacons to receive Bluetooth signals. On the other hand, RFID tags are more related to the possibility for SMEs to know the position of products within stores. This particular use of RFID technology may have two principal outcomes in such a context. First, it may make the management of reassortment procedures easier. A business may know at any moment where products are within the store and how much of them are on scaffolds. Thus, with RFID tags attached to outcomes, SMEs can simply decide to not reassort a platform or a warehouse for some days, as there are still more than enough units of a specific product that consumers may purchase. Second, RFID is fundamental to implementing self-checkout kiosks. Specifically, if shoplifting barriers also have RFID reading capabilities, they may prevent shoplifters from stealing products by cheating on a self-checkout machine.

An example of a successful application of RFID from the retail sector is represented by Macy's case. Accordingly, Macy's implemented RFID technologies throughout all the fashion collections in its store. It emerged how RFID could improve inventory accuracy and reduce the risk of having highly demanded products out-of-stock. In fact, RFID technologies hold the potential to monitor how many products are sold immediately and immediately replenish the shelves. In Macy's case, managers observed how RFID inventory accuracy increased from 63% to 95%. Out-of-stock mistakes were reduced by up to 50% (www.forbes.com).

While Macy's is a huge retail company, the same may apply also to SMEs selling products online. Aside from benefits in the production area, even SMEs may more easily monitor their stocks through these systems. This is particularly truc considering how RFID and RTLS chips frequently cost in the 0.01–0.05$ range, and readers are inexpensive and easy to use.

3.2.3 Mobile Technologies

Mobile technology is made up of portable two-way communication computing devices and the network technology that connects them. Communication networks connecting these devices are called wireless technologies (Krishen et al., 2021). The primary examples are as follows:

1. Cellular Networks: Radio networks using distributed cell towers (cell phones)

2. WiFi: Radio waves that connect devices to the Internet through localized routers called hotspots. Most mobile devices allow automatic switching between WiFi and cellular networks
3. Bluetooth: A telecommunications technology for connecting devices over short distances using shortwave radio waves

In the context of Industry 4.0, mobile devices ensure the reception and processing of large amounts of information on the Internet. They are equipped with high-quality cameras and microphones, which allow them to record and transmit information. The main effects of the diffusion of these tools are as follows:

1. The connectivity of inanimate objects allows companies to communicate with each other.
2. Mobile devices can receive and transmit process-related data in advance and allow users to address issues as they go through real-time decision-making.
3. Mobile devices are now used practically and can interact with process equipment, materials, finished products, and parts via IoT.

Concerning SMEs' future marketing strategies, mobile network importance is twofold. First, they may be used for internal purposes such as monitoring and communication. Second, they may have a role in improving communication with consumers during their purchases. Chats, messages, and photos/videos streamed in real time may attract consumers toward a specific product and may provide this latter additional information. Indeed, most SMEs currently use mobile devices to stream content on the internet. Additionally, those involved in direct selling may provide salespersons with mobile devices to better provide information to consumers and to exchange data.

3.2.4 Cybersecurity Tools

The transformation of Industry 4.0 requires intense data collection and processing activities: the security of data storage and transfer processes is a fundamental concept for companies. Cybersecurity tools, for this reason, are the last necessary basic technology.

Security should be included in cloud technologies, machines, robots, and automated systems by considering the following issues:

1. Data export.
2. Privacy Policy.
3. Personal authorization level for information sharing.
4. Detection and response to unexpected changes and unauthorized access using standardized algorithms.

While large companies have been compliant concerning data security for a long time—policy makers indeed provided regulation for multinational companies about data exchange—in SMEs, it is a new phenomenon (as an example, in Europe, it started to be a diffused practice after the diffusion of the 2016 General Data Protection Regulation, GDPR). In this regard, it emerged how all companies, regardless of their size, must become compliant in terms of data security and prevention of potential breaches of the personal information of consumers.

3.2.5 Internet of Things (IoT)

As stressed in the second paragraph, in the business context, the possibility of implementing IoT as an opportunity for a business involves extending internet-based technologies into existing machines and connecting them to the internet to make these machines exchange data among each other (Del Giudice, 2016). IoT is the first supportive transversal technology allowing us to obtain meaningful information from basic technologies.

Contrary to the digital technologies presented thus far, IoT applications in SME marketing contexts have become popular only over the last decade due to price reductions with respect to the supporting architectures. As assessed the IoT was first adopted mostly in production plants. Indeed, it was easier to produce data from embedded sensors and actuators in production tools than in stores (Caputo et al., 2016). It was derived from the fact that modern production machines were already produced with all the necessary components to enable data exchange. At the same time, it was initially uneconomical to embed IoT connections into most consumer products. Consequently, only some of the original IoT tools were designed for SMEs, particularly for marketing purposes. However, the moment IoT technologies began to be capable of performing different tasks, any business started to pay attention to the IoT. In this moment, SMEs started to pressure IoT developers and producers to rethink the IoT to address their problems.

Accordingly, today IoT has revolutionized several processes existing within SMEs. In detail, first, the IoT is dramatically increasing businesses' supply chain management efficiency. Next, it may reduce labor costs by replacing some categories of employees with receivers that are able to generate the same results. Much of employees' time and energy is focused on keeping track of items to ensure that some products are never out-of-stock and that items are not misplaced on various shelves. Now, because of IoT sensors, it will be possible to identify how many units have been sold at any moment (www.hubspot.com). Third, and consequently, if RFID technologies are used in conjunction with IoT, a business may start to use smart shelves, which are electronically connected shelves that automatically keep track of inventory in a retail store (Loebbecke, 2004).

Then, it is possible to generally assess that the IoT may increase SMEs' marketing tracking efficiency while improving the experience of consumers, as it will allow them always to have awareness of products in stock and replenish shelves.

As proof of the potential of the IoT, McKinsey is predicting that the uses of the IoT will generate additional revenues for businesses between 410$ billion and 1.2$ trillion over the next five years (Manyika, 2015). The impact of the IoT is related to the degree of integration of things connected to the internet in the store. That is, in the case, shelves are connected to the internet. In this regard, something that may prove highly complex is related to the need to foster IoT implementation in SMEs. These businesses may, in fact, be resistant to change and do not perceive the importance of updating their current systems. However, it is extremely difficult to interconnect other technologies without the IoT.

3.2.6 Embedded Systems (Cyber-Physical Systems) and Cloud Systems

The most visible use of computers and software is for information processing for human consumption: we use them to search for information on the web, track financial data, watch videos, and so on. Most computers in use, however, are much less visible They turn on your car's engine, brakes, seat belts, airbags, and audio system. Or they digitally encode your voice and build a radio signal to send it from your mobile phone to a base station. They also check the microwave, refrigerator, and dishwasher.

These less visible computers are called embedded systems, and the software they run is called embedded software. Embedded systems, called *cyber-physical systems (CPSs)*, can be explained as a support technology for organizing and coordinating network systems between their physical infrastructure and computational capabilities. In this regard, physical and digital tools should be integrated and connected with other devices to realize decentralized actions.

In other words, embedded systems generally integrate the physical reality about innovative functionalities, including computing and communication infrastructure.

Most embedded systems rely on devices internally building computation processors. However, whether the task that must be performed requires more power and more computational capability may be connected to external systems that are cloud-based. Cloud computing is a model for enabling ubiquitous, cost-effective, on-demand network access to a shared pool of configurable computing resources (e.g., networks, servers, storage, applications, and services) that can be rapidly provisioned and released with minimal management effort or interaction with the service provider. In Industry 4.0 contexts, 'cloud' includes cloud computing and cloud-based manufacturing and manufacturing process design (Galletta et al., 2017). The main purpose is to improve efficiency by reducing product life cycle costs and enabling the optimal use of resources by coping with customer-oriented jobs with variable demand (flexibility). Cloud-based design and manufacturing operations refer to collective and integrated product development models.

The integration between embedded systems and cloud computing offers tremendous opportunities for SMEs in terms of the application of CPS. First, the embedded systems allow for offline control over the computational process and the possibility to add some script through an interface existing within the business. Second, the cloud can rely on additional computational power if the quantity of data continues to increase while maintaining internal flexibility. Thus, it is possible to implement systems capable of detecting human and machine actions and augmenting their capabilities (Pitsis et al., 2020). Obviously, these systems may provide opportunities for businesses, as they will improve consumers' experience and better foster their purchase intention.

3.2.7 Additive Manufacturing

Additive manufacturing (i.e., 3D printing) is a set of technologies that produce three-dimensional objects directly from digital models through an additive process, specifically by depositing and joining the products with the appropriate polymers, ceramics, or metals.

Additive manufacturing is initiated by developing a computer-aided design (CAD) that lays out a set of digital characteristics of the product and sends the item descriptions to the industrial machines: the machines execute the descriptions transmitted as blueprints to form the item by adding layers of material.

Layers, usually measured in microns, are added to form a three-dimensional object.

Among the productive, supportive technologies, additive manufacturing is the one generating the most significant effects in terms of consumers' satisfaction deriving from products. 3D printing allows the development of almost any kind of product. This technology then enables mass customization. Consumers could imagine a product (or design it if they have enough skills to develop their own design), look after a production point, and then produce it in the real world.

Currently, 3D printer costs are affordable even for SMEs with low budgets. Hence, it represents a possibility to achieve mass customization in a short time.

3.2.8 Robotics Technologies

Industrial robots have been used for over 60 years to automate all types of production lines. Traditional industrial robots are designed for fast and accurate position control; they are perfect for tasks that can be described entirely as a trajectory, such as moving an object from point A to point B, cutting a circle on a metal part, painting a car body, and so on.

The next generation robot must evolve beyond the concept of 'collaboration' to address the root problems. 'Adaptive' is the word that precisely describes the characteristics of the new-generation robot; traditional robots work without adaptability: parts must be in fixed position and orientation; no disturbance is allowed during work.

These principles, as it is possible to observe, originate in the realm of production. However, over the last two decades, robots have found applications within marketing strategies.

On the one hand, the descendants of industrial robots had become assistant robots. These robots started to assist consumers during their in-store experience or buyers' experience within fairs. Robots may bring samples to consumers. Likewise, they could provide information about paths that may need to be followed by consumers. Recently, robots have also started to look like sales assistants bringing products to consumers during their visits. Whether embedded with artificial intelligence (AI), robots can easily be used in human places for tasks such as picking up online orders or managing returns.

Other applications of robots within marketing realms pertain to the use of AI-embedded applications called chatbots. Chatbots are pseudo-robots (as they frequently do not have a physical appearance) that can be used to respond to human requests. Chatbots could assist in nurturing consumers' relationships, as they could respond at any time to questions from humans (even when the shops or businesses are closed). Additionally, these tools may help in the management of e-commerce, as they can provide information to consumers, such as size, price, or delivery methods (Iizuka & Ikeda, 2021).

In the case of SMEs, these businesses could use the first kind of robot to improve the in-store experience or to manage warehouses automatically. Regarding chatbots, they may provide valuable help if they are needed to manage e-commerce with low costs. In such a regard, SMEs may also rely on key partners to provide intelligent solutions to support the implementation of chatbots (Kushwaha et al., 2021). Key partners may manage the development and the solving of common software glitches.

3.2.9 Virtualization Techniques (Virtual Reality, Augmented Reality, and Simulation Techniques)

Virtual reality (VR) is an ensemble of computer-generated stimuli capable of making an individual perceive a simulated digital world as the real one. A VR instrument is then an item that can generate a digital image/world good enough to make a person believe that such a digital image/world is real or extremely like the actual image/world. Usually, technologies to make a person undergo a VR experience are based on visors, head cuffs, gloves, and displays. Accordingly, the scope of implementing virtual reality is to alienate a person from the real world and make him/her holistically experience a virtual world.

Augment reality (AR) is an interactive experience of the real world where real-world objects are 'augmented' by computer-generated inputs. Hence, any item endowed with a digital camera and a screen to project the augmented images may represent an appropriate tool to make a person experience AR. Consequently, the scope of the implementation of augmented reality is to create a person experience the real world while receiving additional digital information (Nantel, 2004).

While the implementation of two such technologies will have different effects, both have emerged as the most long-standing disruptive digital innovations in the marketing context. VR was the first one to appear. It first emerged as virtual stores where consumers may move around to select and purchase new products. Then, VR materialized in the e-commerce realm before being used in the traditional SME realm (Roggeveen et al., 2016). Originally, VR applications were limited to now-outdated virtual stores offering consumers and were receiving communications from a virtual sales assistant. The possibility of interacting with products was thereby quite limited.

Because of the evolution of software, additional capabilities were added to VR applications. As an example, fashion e-tailers started offering consumers the possibility to insert their body measurements online and provide them with a mock-up regarding how the dress will fit. It was at this moment that traditional businesses started to integrate virtual reality into their newly developed online platforms. In fact, by doing so, traditional businesses finally found themselves capable of competing with full e-tailers by offering the possibility to consumers to evaluate a product online and purchase it online or in the physical store (Suh & Lee, 2005).

Regarding practical VR applications, the use of VR by IKEA is undoubtedly remarkable. As is possible to observe, IKEA is starting to develop within some of the stores' VR corners. In such places, customers may try to immerse themselves into a complete product usage experience, thus being more aware about what they are going to purchase (www.ikea.com).

AR, on the other hand, emerged as a technology capable of disrupting businesses' ways of doing business only recently. To implement AR-based tools, it was necessary to await the diffusion of smartphones or new-generation tablets. As AR is based on screen- and camera-endowed portable devices, only nowadays businesses start to consider them as a concrete strategic opportunity (Dennis et al., 2012). Specifically, over recent years, it emerged how consumers' experience may be enriched by providing them information (i.e., price, product specifications, location of similar products) on the screen of portable devices. In addition, it emerged that suggesting individuals customized promotions based on their preferences was a proper strategy to incentivize people to purchase more products.

Some interesting cases of applications of AR in stores can be traced in the apparel industry. From this perspective, on the one hand, it was observed how some chains, such as Timberland started to implement technologies offering customers the possibility to observe how something is fitting on them. On the other hand, other ones, such as Lacoste are diffusing AR applications for smartphones showing customers prices and promotions (www.shopify.com).

In recent times, AR and VR have become pillars of the so-called Metaverse. The expression Metaverse may be used to describe any virtual environment that allows for brand-consumer interactions through the avatars of the latter. It is based on AR and VR, as it is necessary to develop a completely new virtual environment where brand-generated content exists and may be experienced by consumers. In the Metaverse, consumers may also purchase digital products, which could either complement their real-world purchase (i.e., the digital twin of an actual product) or substitute it (i.e., a product based on NFT certificates that exist only in the digital environment). Even for SMEs, AR, VR, or the Metaverse could represent a huge opportunity, albeit their actual application is still far away. They could develop digital stores or showrooms to attract distant consumers. Otherwise, more traditionally, they could develop AR-based applications to show a product's size and features to any consumer. This notwithstanding, accessing the metaverse is currently still difficult for SMEs. The evolution of the underlying technologies (even concerning ease of use) will then represent the cutting edge in making these environments accessible even for SMEs.

3.2.10 Big Data Analytics, Machine Learning and Artificial Intelligence

Machine learning is the set of techniques that allows a computer to learn new ways to accomplish or optimize the execution of a task through progressive and cumulative data collection and analysis. A machine embedded with machine learning capabilities may discover a new and more efficient way to conduct an analysis because of the iterative replication of the same computation process over time. Artificial intelligence, instead, is a form of intelligence that machines may demonstrate. Machines endowed by artificial intelligence may transform from a traditional passive item into an artificial cognitive system. Artificial intelligence-endowed machines will then be capable of deciding autonomously how to perform a task and how to plan their daily activities (Rialti, Marzi et al., 2018).

The possibility of businesses relying on analytics systems bestowed by machine learning capabilities or artificial intelligence represents another relevant disruptive factor. On the one hand, machines characterized by artificial intelligence can be fundamental to increasing businesses' degree of automation in any processes. Such devices will be able to act autonomously to maximize a preset outcome without human intervention. For instance, regarding the assembly of an order made by consumers, machines endowed by artificial intelligence can pick up goods from the warehouse and put them in delivery boxes (www.techemergence.com).

On the other hand, such machines endowed with machine learning capabilities offer the opportunity for businesses to obtain a whole new level of detailed knowledge about their consumers (Hofacker et al., 2016). Due to machine learning, computers can now perform more detailed data analysis (including big data) every time. Hence, in the second or third iteration of an analytics process, they may be able to identify consumers' behavioral patterns or specific insights that were not identified during the first round. This is possible because machine learning-capable machines rely on unsupervised statistical analysis methods, which are focused on the identification of commonalities in unstructured data and react based on the presence or absence of such commonalities in each new piece. Thus, businesses may now have their databases processed by a machine learning endowed machine and get new insights from usual data about consumers without performing any additional tasks. Because most of these new insights will be about consumers' behavior and preferences, this further information may be used by businesses to develop consumer-tailored marketing strategies, such as micromarketing strategies (Erevelles et al., 2016). Another example of an artificial intelligence application may be related to a new generation of shopping assistants. In fact, digital shopping assistants are, in effect, just digital technologies capable of replying to a natural language question owing to their ability to interpret a question in human language and respond accordingly (Kaplan & Haenlein, 2018). Artificial intelligence-based technologies can therefore contribute toward the improvement of consumers' in-store and outside-store experience, either by providing them with more information inside the store or by enacting the SME to offer customized services more adherent to consumers' preferences.

AI is one of the enablers of the correct functioning of all the other technologies in synchrony. AI is the brain behind all the other tools, while data are the nutrients. The more AI is capable of learning about business processes, the merrier will be the implementation of I4.0

technologies in marketing (Tiwari et al., 2021). In the case of SMEs, AI may be implemented through outsourced solutions. Some of the most relevant providers of AI solutions are Google and Amazon (AWS). Setting a genetic algorithm may challenge SMEs; skills are frequently low in such aspects. Hence, relying on a new workforce or consultants that could develop a suitable solution is fundamental. Additionally, SME managers may feel hostility toward AI and AI-based decisions, as they usually tend to concentrate decision processes in their hands (Liu et al., 2021). However, if these resistances are overcome, AI may allow learning more about processes and consumers. AI may also prove fundamental to improving the forecasting capabilities of SMEs; thus, these businesses may better predict future market trends and may manage production accordingly.

3.2.11 Blockchain and Smart Contracts

Blockchain is an open and distributed public ledger that can be used by two parties to register a transaction occurring in a digital environment in a permanent and unmodifiable way. The effectivity of blockchain resides in the mechanism it works. First, the seller of some products creates the first block of the chain; every time someone purchases one, the blockchain provider creates a new block containing the transaction details. Therefore, due to blockchain, it will be possible to trace back all the transactions concerning an item. Additionally, as the provider acts as a trusted authority of the chain, it is impossible for the seller to double-spend or to try to sell the product twice.

In its very first form, it was invented by Satoshi Nakamoto as the public ledger for bitcoin transactions. However, businesses have started developing their own digital ledgers to register product-related transactions every day. The contracts such transactions usually rely on fall within the smart contracts category, which are self-executing contracts with the terms of agreement between buyer and seller being directly written into lines of the digital codes. Such contracts are currently among the most secure, as they provide the transfer of a specific good only after the sum of money is received by the seller, yet they also protect the buyer, as the sum of money will be automatically reimbursed if the seller is not capable of shipping the product (Iansiti & Lakhani, 2017).

Blockchain is one of the most innovative digital trends that will affect SMEs. If businesses implement private blockchains, then it will be possible for them to improve the way they are conducting online transactions. This may generate two effects. First, it may allow businesses to trace (and make more secure) all the transactions deriving from supplying processes. The moment a business purchases a good from a supplier, the transaction will be registered permanently in the online ledger; thus, it will be possible to monitor all the information and transaction costs related to that item. As such, blockchain may improve supply chain efficiency (Xu et al., 2017). Second, internal blockchains may dramatically affect B2C exchanges occurring online. Blockchain-based e-commerce platforms will, in fact, make purchase processes easier and safer for consumers. Notably, due to blockchain, consumers can complete a transaction with just a few clicks and be protected from scams due to the smart contract underlying the transaction mentioned above. On the one hand, the smart contract ensures that the business may receive the agreed sum. On the other hand, the marketing registered on the ledger may help the SME to monitor all the transactions occurring (Kshetri, 2017).

Blockchain, however, still needs to show all its possible applications and its potential. However, building on these conceptual premises, may dramatically affect any industry. Examples of its usage are common in many business areas, such as e-commerce. Indeed, e-tailers are investing more than any other business category in blockchain to make customers' payments safer, register all transactions, and make them easily consultable in the case of managers' needs (www.smartereum.com).

In sum, for SMEs, blockchain offers two principal opportunities. The first concerns the possibility of striking a balance in e-commerce relationships. SMEs may use blockchain to manage their online transactions, thus tracing who the consumers are, obtaining more data, and ensuring their payment mechanisms on e-tailer platforms. The second application concerns the possibility of selling digital products online. Digital products (corresponding to an NFT protocol explaining the current and the previous owners of the product) may extend SMEs' revenue channels, as businesses currently may also sell digital ideas or digital developments as real products.

3.2.12 Digital Payments

As hinted by the description of AR technologies and smart beacons, consumers' possession of their digital tools is something that SMEs are taking very seriously. Consumers' private digital tools such as smartphones, tablets, and similar stuff may revolutionize how consumers behave within the store or change their out-of-store habits.

First, mobile technologies are potential enablers of the implementation of AR and smart beacons, and they may dramatically change consumers' in-store experience. In particular, because of mobile tools, consumers may now receive a vast quantity of information about stores, products, and promotions. As consumers' in-store experience is related to the ease with which they will be able to complete their tasks, the possibility of relying on devices capable of suggesting to them where the products are may reduce their time in the shop while making them able to find (and purchase) more products. The possibility of receiving customized advertising is also useful, as it will make consumers feel 'exclusive', thus potentially fostering their loyalty.

Second, mobility is revolutionizing how consumers obtain the goods they seek. In fact, using new smartphone apps, consumers may now purchase products at home and pick them up in-store after checking them. This will provide several advantages for both companies and consumers. Companies, in fact, may save money on shipping costs procedures (in the case they provide free shipping) or to what concerns returns (consumers may decide not to collect a product by leaving it in the store or by changing it for another product while in the store). Second, thanks to the implementation of buy online, pick up in-store systems, consumers will still have to go to the physical store; thus, they may look at other products and decide to purchase more goods or ask for additional services. Consumers may find better promotions online. In addition, they may avoid looking for items in the store, which may be quite annoying if they do not find something they want. Finally, consumers may avoid queues for checkout, thanks to employees checking up their smartphones to validate the handover of the products.

Third, mobile technologies are currently providing consumers the opportunity to pay for their products without using physical money. Such a mechanism has been defined as mobile POS or smart payment. While it may not seem a huge change for both businesses and consumers, in some countries, this novelty has caused a significant effect on both SMEs' management of cash and consumers' experience. Specifically, companies are allowed the direct transfer of money in their bank account without any intermediation (i.e., security services or bank costs). To what concerns consumers, this specific technology is making payments safer, easier, and faster. Consequently, it also allows them to check out from the store quickly, thus improving the in-store experience (Taylor, 2016).

Examples of the applications of these technologies within the retail sector are luckily clearly visible to most customers. Indeed, most current businesses currently allow customers to purchase online and pick up products in-store. Similarly, most large-scale firms are already implementing automatic checkouts both to make customers' experience better and to save on salesforce costs (Faraoni, Rialti, Zollo, & Pellicelli, 2018).

In terms of future trends deriving from mobile payments, it is relevant to evidence cryptocurrency-enabled payment and buy now pay later platforms. Cryptocurrencies such as Bitcoin, Doge, and Ethereum (just to name a few) are digital money that can be purchased by consumers in exchange for traditional currencies. Cryptocurrencies may be collected by consumers in digital wallets to pay for their online purchases. Cryptocurrencies present some advantages for businesses, as wallets are safe, and their value is objective and may be checked by the seller (Thampanya et al., 2020). Digital wallets, additionally, transmit more information to the buyer than a credit card to the seller. However, such instruments of payment also present some challenges, as businesses will need to trace such payments and adopt tools to convert cryptocurrencies into traditional currencies. Buy now pay later (BNPL) platforms are intermediaries between consumers and businesses and allow payment to be deferred to a second moment. The seller obtains the correct amount immediately, while the buyer may pay in more tranches. These instruments require just the creation of an account for both involved parties but may allow a consumer to immediately satisfy their purchase intention (Chen et al., 2021).

SMEs will need to be ready to adapt to all these changes. Allowing consumers to pay through different and multiple methods may enable these businesses to attract a growing number of consumers (in particular from younger generations). Just the availability of more than one method may influence the willingness of some consumers to select a seller with respect to another. Additionally, consumers are more prone to convert their purchase stimulus into an actual purchase as they can pay with 'whatever they have at their hand'.

3.3 How Technologies 4.0 Are Affecting SMES' Business Model and Marketing Strategies

The way SMEs operate and get in touch with consumers can radically change in the 4.0 era. These technologies are disruptive and may affect how processes are run and marketing campaigns are developed. In this regard, adopting I4.0 technologies could influence how businesses, including SMEs, create value (Matthyssens, 2019). The increased control over information allows us to reconfigure the production side better. Companies may consistently increase their efficiency and use fewer resources to obtain strategic objectives. However, businesses could also improve their effectiveness in achieving their mission. Whether technologies are applied on the marketing side, businesses may better be in touch with consumers, reduce time-to-market, and better trace payments (Scuotto et al., 2021).

Diverse technologies may generate different effects. Obviously, much of the possible outcomes of 4.0-driven digital transformation derive from the company's objectives and the application area. SMEs already operating in e-commerce may benefit from the implementation of BDA or AI to better analyze their existing consumer data. Thus, these businesses may rely on external providers of these solutions to improve internal knowledge about their consumers (Chen et al., 2021). SMEs experiencing warehouse and stock problems (i.e., lower than expected stock levels and the impossibility of supplying consumers) may instead benefit from the application of RFID and traceability technologies in conjunction with blockchain (Bag et al., 2021). SMEs with outstanding credits may benefit from BNPL solutions allowing consumers to pay in separate tranches. However, SMEs with many consumers in distant countries may benefit from digital showrooms where it may be possible to show products thanks to AR or VR.

In such regards, something businesses should consider in conjunction with technological choice concerns the pillars of 4.0-oriented business models. These pillars should drive SMEs from the technological selection phase and must be integrated into the decision framework regarding how technologies should work.

The seven pillars are as follows:

a. **Interoperability** implies the communication framework that will be developed to create a smart business. In detail, seeking interoperability means that any company wishing to integrate a new technology needs to observe how it is going to fit within the existing business objectives and about existing and expected future technologies.
b. **Virtualization**, which allows monitoring of the entire system, readaptation of the system, and modifications to the system itself. Virtualization then pertains to the possibility and the willingness to virtualize the control of different processes and to adapt it to different situations that the business may encounter.
c. **Decentralization** is a key term for achieving autonomous decision-making of machines and is based on learning from previous events and actions. Whether a business seeks digitalization, it is necessary to rely on autonomous decisions from machines, thus decentralizing decisions previously centered on managers.
d. **Real-time data management** is the 'track and trace' of the system. Switching from time-to-time to real-time systems for SMEs denotes the need to develop new information systems and to completely change the data management 'philosophy' by starting to collect all the possible information to feed AI (Bag et al., 2021).

e. **Service orientation** is the adaptation to customer needs of the whole system integrating internal and external subsystems.
f. **Integrated business processes,** which represent the outcome of interoperability. Indeed, such an approach concerns communication and coordination mechanisms within intelligent businesses.
g. **Agility and flexibility**, which means that the business has become a system capable of adapting to changing needs through internal reconfiguration.

What emerges from this evidence, then, is that SMEs wishing to embrace the 4.0 world will need to change paradigmatically. Some traditional approaches adopted by businesses will need to be completely transformed and, in some cases, completely abandoned. Going digital is a process that requires changes in decision-making systems and increased reliance on information.

This notwithstanding, in the case that a business can achieve the expected objectives, the impact on its business models may be remarkable. While these are just examples of what may occur to SMEs, the following area of business models may be affected:

1. **Key partners:** Several new key partners may emerge for SMEs following a 4.0 strategy. For example, cloud solution providers, AI platforms, and infrastructure maintenance partners are fundamental to ensure the system's functioning (Tiwari et al., 2021). Likewise, SMEs may need to look after reliable partners to which they outsource some of the data analytics activities.
2. **Key activities and resources:** The adoption of a 4.0-oriented paradigm will make data processing activities as important as productive ones. Consistently, data are becoming critical resources within the business. Through data, businesses will currently manage all future changes and future needs. Henceforth, collecting, cleansing, storing, and analyzing data will have a pivotal role.
3. **Value proposition:** Innovative offerings may be developed by businesses through the analysis of consumer preferences. In this regard, it is relevant to consider how data may stimulate the process of open innovation. Consumers may then co-create value with businesses.

Consequently, companies may increase their sales and their revenues (Matthyssens, 2019). It needs to be kept in mind that SMEs frequently lack research resources to develop innovative consumer-driven solutions, and technologies such as BDA and AI may allow them to enter this real at low cost. Additionally, through 4.0 solutions such as 3D printing, it may be possible to offer a completely new range of customized products.

4. **Consumers' relationship, channels, and new consumer segments:** 4.0 technologies provide the opportunity to reach new consumers and to nurture relationships with existing ones. In such a regard, first, it is fundamental to consider that through data, it is possible even for SMEs to provide consumers with the right information (or the right reply) at the right time. Likewise, it is possible to know better than ever consumers interested in our products, and maybe a new consumer segment may emerge.
5. **Cost structure and revenue streams:** Thanks to data, it is possible for SMEs to spend better and better invest money. It may become possible to understand bottlenecks in production and inefficiencies and quantify stocks in the warehouse. As previously assessed, data may increase business efficiency. New revenues may instead be achieved through better market penetration and customized marketing strategies (De Luca et al., 2021).

3.3.1 The Impact of Technologies 4.0 on Business Models

New technologies influence the way businesses are creating value. Their impact, however, has proven so huge that entirely new business models started to emerge. Some businesses (including SMEs) reached an extremely high level of digital readiness in which the way they were operating could not be described through traditional representations.

To describe the ways these companies create value, four new business model archetypes have been defined: integration, servitization, expertise as service, and marketization (Ustundag & Cevikcan, 2017).

a. **Integration:** Integration is a form of business model innovation that includes a 'value chain orchestrator' and an 'integrator'. An orchestrator is highly specialized on a single step of the value chain, while an integrator aims to cover the entire value chain. SMEs could maintain either role according to their core business. However, what is emerging is that we are currently in an era in which interactions with consumers are moving from indirect through intermediaries to direct customers through online platforms. Innovation is switching toward open-innovation processes by integrating customers and other external partners in product development. In this regard, such a kind of business model innovation pertains to businesses, regardless of the level of specialization, that may integrate 'digitally' more production phases. Whether businesses are orchestrators (thus specialized in one production phase), they may overcome their production limitations through the 'virtual' integration of additional phases. Businesses that are integrators could instead improve their linkages with the market through the platforms and develop new relationships. Integrative innovation, then, explains how SMEs could obtain increased benefits due to the possibility of integrating value chains digitally.

   Integration is based on the notion of platform in which orchestrator and integrator coexist and in which the first manages the interactions and associates the latter with potential customers. Their sub-archetypes may exist:

- *Crowd Sourcing-Based Integration*, which describes how intelligence and information are harnessed from the crowd by SMEs through platforms.
- *Production as Service*, which is a sub-archetype explaining how a business may cover just a producing position within in the supply chain and be contacted through the platform by anyone interested in production capacity.
- *Mass customization* is a sub-archetype providing that SMEs provide both production capacity and design capabilities and offer both to consumers wishing to create new customized products. 3D printing centers represent a common example of such businesses.

b. **Servitization:** The integration of sensors and Wi-Fi connections into products enables new product assistance systems. Businesses are currently not just selling tangible products; they are selling bundles of products and post-sales services enabled by 4.0 technologies. Therefore, additional new services rather than new products are the basis of this business model innovation.

   Servitization provides complementary services to the traditional sale of products. While similar business models also existed in the past (i.e., companies were selling products and additional services such as insurance), thanks to 4.0 technologies, it is possible to develop lifelong partnerships and replace traditional product sales with services that include a product (product as service and result as service) eliminate the high investment costs for customers (buying only one service) and, therefore, target new customer segments. As it is possible to suggest, 4.0 technologies play a pivotal role in enabling this new business model. These technologies enable data exchange between products and businesses, thus allowing businesses to understand better what is happening to a product and providing exact assistance at the right moment.
c. **Expertise as service:** This model postulates businesses exploit internally acquired product or process expertise and offers it as a new consultancy service or new product to external customers. Consulting service shifts the value chain focus to service and support, requiring consultants' human role as key assets. The firm's role shifts up the value chain toward an intermediary and creates a multifaceted market. Value capture then evolves from one-time sales to ongoing subscription fees. The main forms are product consulting, process consulting, brokerage platform management, and continuous service provision. In the case of SMEs, many are operating directly in 4.0 consulting; otherwise, they offer subscriptions for the use of software enabling the functioning of other technologies.
d. **Marketization:** The last archetypes allow businesses to exploit 4.0 technologies to increase their market reach, improve consumer relationships, position their products at the top of consumer preferences, customize products, and expand the range of experience that consumers may live during their usage of the product, and consistently monitor

all feedback from consumers. Such a model is theoretically an extremization of business market orientation; however, the future for many companies is represented by the pursuit of such a possibility. Increasing the contact with the market is a matter of life or death for many SMEs operating either in the B2B or B2C contexts (Ardito et al., 2018).

3.3.2 Marketing Strategists in the 4.0 Landscape: How to Lever New Technologies

Marketing has significantly evolved in recent decades. Scholars agree that four main phases characterized the recent evolution of marketing: Marketing 1.0 (product-centric), Marketing 2.0 (consumer-centric), Marketing 3.0 (human-centric), and Marketing 4.0 (digital-centric) (see Dash et al., 2021).

Marketing 1.0 was focused on creating the best product (or service) of the market, meaning better than the already existing alternatives provided by competitors. Hence, marketers used differentiation strategies most (Dickson & Ginter, 1987). The main critical issue is the way companies approached the targeted audience; by overly focusing on the product's features and distinctive elements, the main goal was often neglected: to satisfy customers' needs and meet their expectations. However, how is this possible if the ultimate objective is beating the competition to increase market share? Although a product's features are one of the most important elements in new product development (NPD) effectiveness (Bianchi et al., 2019), the starting point must be redesigned. Actually, 'product is king' is no more a suitable strategy because it makes marketers and developers focus mainly on the *means* through which satisfying customers' needs and exceed expectations. In this way, the *goal* is neglected or not prioritized. This old paradigm might lead to an excessive 'technology-push' approach, ignoring the market's actual requirements (Marzi et al., 2016). As a result, many investments in developing the 'best' product were deemed a failure, showing few returns and market success. Marketers should have answered the question: 'best for whom'?

Marketing 2.0 represented the necessary shift of the old paradigm. Marketers started developing product design and market penetration strategies by emphasizing customers' and consumers' desires in the first stage. From a 'technology-push' approach, strategists discovered the effectiveness of a 'market-pull' orientation (Pellegrini et al., 2019), meaning that the need to solve a specific customer's pain point came directly from the market and not from the company. In this way, marketers were able to ideate and develop products as real solutions (i.e., *painkillers*) for their targeted customers. The go-to-market strategy becomes customer-centric by focusing on the main gaps perceived by the market in terms of solutions to an existing problem that has not yet been fully satisfied. One of the main benefits of such an approach refers to avoid wasting time and resources in designing and developing products for already saturated markets, meaning that no real need is expressed by customers. Moreover, the risk of being perceived as a company providing 'vitamin pills'—adding new features to existing solutions—and not concrete painkillers might be avoided in this way (Kirk & Zollo, 2021). However, this paradigmatic shift was not enough for companies to be perceived as the market leader or to be perfectly positioned in customers' minds.

Marketing 3.0 is mostly related to the servitization revolution (Kowalkowski et al., 2017), which allowed marketers to interpret consumers as 'human beings, thus focusing on providing no more than a single product *una tantum* but offering a full service of solutions across a wider and longer lifespan. The main goal here is nurturing an emotional and rational connection among companies' brands and customers. Creating a 'human' relationship with customers allows several benefits, such as (1) increasing LTV (lifetime value), (2) studying changes in consumers' preferences, attitudes, and behaviors during a range of time, and (3) solving different pain points with one single service (no more a specific problem with a specific solution). Let us consider Spotify, which is not perceived as a single product, but as a servitization platform able to solve several music lovers' pains; most importantly, the greater the listener remains in the platform using Spotify's service, the better is the experience in terms of customization, satisfaction, and in turn intention to stay. By transforming brands into tailored services able to provide customers with a long-lasting satisfying experience, marketers could achieve an important equation: *brand identity* = *brand image* (Ranfagni et al., 2021). In other words, the way a company's brand wants to be perceived by the market (i.e., brand identity, composed of values, culture, style, personality, heritage, etc.) will be aligned with the way customers and the market in general perceive the brand image (perceptions and reactions about the brand's presence in a specific need).

Finally, Marketing 4.0 builds on the previous human-centric approach by adding digital transformation and new technological innovations to the brand-customer relationship. Above all, what has changed in the relationship are mainly touchpoints (i.e., interactions and linkages among a company and its customers), which are no longer offline and online but literally pervade all the aspects of consumers' daily lives (Faraoni, Rialti, Zollo, & Pellicelli, 2018). Hence, in an omnichannel approach, marketing strategists provide consumers with a seamless brand experience through several traditional and digital devices (mobiles, apps, social media, videogames, etc.). From this perspective, *brandification* means the constant and, hopefully, fitting presence of brands in consumers' daily activities (Lucarelli & Hallin, 2015). It emerges that brands might be constantly and coherently present in their customers' lives thanks to digital technologies. However, digitalizing companies' products and services is not a competitive asset *per se*. Still, it has to become the instrument through which brands dynamically interact with their target audience, no more in a physical shop but in every step of the customer journey, from the awareness stage to the post-purchase stage. The elements above of Industry 4.0 make this revolution possible; think about Web 3.0, big data, and IoT: these are strategic opportunities for marketers that might better understand their targeted audience needs and behaviors across the (digital) journey (i.e., awareness, consideration, decision, purchase, and post-purchase) and provide offline/online touchpoints step-by-step to walk the consumer toward their physical/digital presence (Lemon & Verhoef, 2016). Specifically, digital platforms and new technologies allow a better personalization and tailorization of products and services, which was impossible before I4.0.

Similarly, just think it is currently more accessible for a company to reach a wider audience thanks to digital channels, such as social media. Digital marketing tools such as Google Analytics allow strategists to assess the exact amount of time (minutes and seconds) a consumer visits an online store or even how many times the company's website is abandoned (bounce rate). These are only a few examples to show how Key Performance

Indicators (KPIs) (i.e., clicks, visits, or conversion optimization) might be improved through digital tools. Therefore, we need to remember that the digital transformation of I4.0 does not represent the revolution of modern marketing, but it is a strategic and practical vehicle to redesign interactions and relationships among companies and customers (see Pratesi et al., 2021).

However, one question remains: how might these marketing shifts be implemented in SMEs, given all the obstacles and difficulties of their digital transformation process?

We will try to explore this issue in the next chapter.

References

Ardito, L., Petruzzelli, A. M., Panniello, U., & Garavelli, A. C. (2018). Towards Industry 4.0: Mapping digital technologies for supply chain management-marketing integration. *Business Process Management Journal, 25*(2), 323–346.

Bag, S., Gupta, S., Kumar, A., & Sivarajah, U. (2021). An integrated artificial intelligence framework for knowledge creation and B2B marketing rational decision making for improving firm performance. *Industrial Marketing Management, 92*, 178–189.

Bianchi, M., Marzi, G., Zollo, L., & Patrucco, A. (2019). Developing software beyond customer needs and plans: An exploratory study of its forms and individual-level drivers. *International Journal of Production Research, 57*(22), 7189–7208.

Caputo, A., Marzi, G., & Pellegrini, M. M. (2016). The internet of things in manufacturing innovation processes: Development and application of a conceptual framework. *Business Process Management Journal, 22*(2), 383–402.

Chen, Y., Richter, J. I., & Patel, P. C. (2021). Decentralized governance of digital platforms. *Journal of Management, 47*(5), 1305–1337.

Chiu, C. Y., Chen, S., & Chen, C. L. (2017). An integrated perspective of TOE framework and innovation diffusion in broadband mobile applications adoption by enterprises. *International Journal of Management, Economics and Social Sciences (IJMESS), 6*(1), 14–39.

Dash, G., Kiefer, K., & Paul, J. (2021). Marketing-to-millennials: Marketing 4.0, customer satisfaction and purchase intention. *Journal of Business Research, 122*, 608–620.

De Luca, L. M., Herhausen, D., Troilo, G., & Rossi, A. (2021). How and when do big data investments pay off? The role of marketing affordances and service innovation. *Journal of the Academy of Marketing Science, 49*(4), 790–810.
Del Giudice, M. (2016). Discovering the internet of things (IoT) within the business process management: A literature review on technological revitalization. *Business Process Management Journal, 22*(2), 263–270.
Delone, W. H., & Mclean, E. R. (2004). Measuring e-commerce success: Applying the DeLone & McLean information systems success model. *International Journal of Electronic Commerce, 9*(1), 31–47.
Dennis, C., Michon, R., Brakus, J. J., Newman, A., & Alamanos, E. (2012). New insights into the impact of digital signage as a retail atmospheric tool. *Journal of Consumer Behaviour, 11*(6), 454–466.
Dickson, P. R., & Ginter, J. L. (1987). Market segmentation, product differentiation, and marketing strategy. *Journal of Marketing, 51*(2), 1–10.
Erevelles, S., Fukawa, N., & Swayne, L. (2016). Big Data consumer analytics and the transformation of marketing. *Journal of Business Research, 69*(2), 897–904.
Faraoni, M., Rialti, R., Zollo, L., & Pellicelli, A. C. (2018). Exploring e-loyalty antecedents in B2C e-commerce: Empirical results from Italian grocery retailers. *British Food Journal*. https://doi.org/10.1108/BFJ-04-2018-0216
Fulgoni, G. M. (2014). "Omni-Channel" retail insights and the consumer's path-to-purchase: How digital has transformed the way people make purchasing decisions. *Journal of Advertising Research, 54*(4), 377–380.
Galletta, A., Carnevale, L., Celesti, A., Fazio, M., & Villari, M. (2017). A cloud-based system for improving retention marketing loyalty programs in industry 4.0: A study on big data storage implications. *IEEE Access, 6*, 5485–5492.
Hofacker, C. F., Malthouse, E. C., & Sultan, F. (2016). Big data and consumer behavior: Imminent opportunities. *Journal of Consumer Marketing, 33*(2), 89–97.
Iansiti, M., & Lakhani, K. R. (2017). The truth about blockchain. *Harvard Business Review, 95*(1), 118–127.
Iizuka, M., & Ikeda, Y. (2021). Regulation and innovation under the 4th industrial revolution: The case of a healthcare robot, HAL by Cyberdyne. *Technovation, 108*, 102335.
Kaplan, A., & Haenlein, M. (2018). Siri, Siri, in my hand: Who's the fairest in the land? On the interpretations, illustrations, and implications of artificial intelligence. *Business Horizons*. https://doi.org/10.1016/j.bushor.2018.08.004

Kehoe, D., & Boughton, N. (2001). Internet based supply chain management: A classification of approaches to manufacturing planning and control. *International Journal of Operations & Production Management, 21*(4), 516–525.

Kirk, N. H., & Zollo, L. (2021). *European Venture Toolbox: The path for SMEs to grasp and defend opportunities*. Emerald Group Publishing.

Kowalkowski, C., Gebauer, H., Kamp, B., & Parry, G. (2017). Servitization and deservitization: Overview, concepts, and definitions. *Industrial Marketing Management, 60*, 4–10.

Krishen, A. S., Dwivedi, Y. K., Bindu, N., & Kumar, K. S. (2021). A broad overview of interactive digital marketing: A bibliometric network analysis. *Journal of Business Research, 131*, 183–195.

Kshetri, N. (2017). Can blockchain strengthen the internet of things? *IT Professional, 19*(4), 68–72.

Kushwaha, A. K., Kumar, P., & Kar, A. K. (2021). What impacts customer experience for B2B enterprises on using AI-enabled chatbots? Insights from Big data analytics. *Industrial Marketing Management, 98*, 207–221.

Lemon, K. N., & Verhoef, P. C. (2016). Understanding customer experience throughout the customer journey. *Journal of Marketing, 80*(6), 69–96.

Liu, X., Shin, H., & Burns, A. C. (2021). Examining the impact of luxury brand's social media marketing on customer engagement: Using big data analytics and natural language processing. *Journal of Business Research, 125*, 815–826.

Loebbecke, C. (2004). Modernizing retailing world at the point of sale. *MIS Quarterly Executive, 3*(4), 242–263.

Lucarelli, A., & Hallin, A. (2015). Brand transformation: A performative approach to brand regeneration. *Journal of Marketing Management, 31*(1–2), 84–106.

Manyika, J. (2015). *The internet of things: Mapping the value beyond the hype*. McKinsey Global Institute. https://www.mckinsey.com/~/media/McKinsey/Business%20Functions/McKinsey%20Digital/Our%20Insights/The%20Internet%20of%20Things%20The%20value%20of%20digitizing%20the%20physical%20world/The-Internet-of-things-Mapping-the-value-beyond-the-hype.ashx

Marzi, G., Marsocci, M., Zollo, L., & Boccardi, A. (2016). Comprendere gli elementi intangibili dell'esperienza turistica heritage: una ricerca netnografica. *Il Capitale Culturale, 13*, 267–297.

Matthyssens, P. (2019). Reconceptualizing value innovation for Industry 4.0 and the industrial internet of things. *The Journal of Business and Industrial Marketing, 34*(6), 1203–1209.

Nantel, J. (2004). My virtual model: Virtual reality comes into fashion. *Journal of Interactive Marketing, 18*(3), 73–86.

Pellegrini, M. M., Marzi, G., Zollo, L., & Ratten, V. (2019). Understanding the role of heritage tourist experience: A netnographic research in Italy. In *Tourism Innovation* (pp. 45–65). Routledge.

Pitsis, T. S., Beckman, S. L., Steinert, M., Oviedo, L., & Maisch, B. (2020). Designing the future: Strategy, design, and the 4th industrial revolution—an introduction to the special issue. *California Management Review, 62*(2), 5–11.

Pratesi, F., Hu, L., Rialti, R., Zollo, L., & Faraoni, M. (2021). Cultural dimensions in online purchase behavior: Evidence from a cross-cultural study. *Italian Journal of Marketing, 3*, 227–247.

Ranfagni, S., Faraoni, M., Zollo, L., & Vannucci, V. (2021). Combining online market research methods for investigating brand alignment: The case of Nespresso. *British Food Journal, 123*(13), 37–58.

Rialti, R., Marzi, G., Ciappei, C., & Caputo, A. (2018). Reframing agile organization. Does big data analytics capabilities matter?. *Academy of Management Global Proceedings, Surrey*, 1–8.

Roggeveen, A. L., Nordfält, J., & Grewal, D. (2016). Do digital displays enhance sales? Role of retail format and message content. *Journal of Retailing, 92*(1), 122–131.

Scuotto, V., Nicotra, M., Del Giudice, M., Krueger, N., & Gregori, G. L. (2021). A microfoundational perspective on SMEs' growth in the digital transformation era. *Journal of Business Research, 129*, 382–392.

Suh, K. S., & Lee, Y. E. (2005). The effects of virtual reality on consumer learning: An empirical investigation. *Mis Quarterly, 36*, 673–697.

Taylor, E. (2016). Mobile payment technologies in retail: A review of potential benefits and risks. *International Journal of Retail & Distribution Management, 44*(2), 159–177.

Thampanya, N., Nasir, M. A., & Huynh, T. L. D. (2020). Asymmetric correlation and hedging effectiveness of gold & cryptocurrencies: From pre-industrial to the 4th industrial revolution. *Technological Forecasting and Social Change, 159*, 120195.

Tiwari, A. K., Abakah, E. J. A., Le, T. L., & Leyva-de la Hiz, D. I. (2021). Markov-switching dependence between artificial intelligence and carbon price: The role of policy uncertainty in the era of the 4th industrial revolution

and the effect of COVID-19 pandemic. *Technological Forecasting and Social Change, 163*, 120434.
Ustundag, A., & Cevikcan, E. (2017). *Industry 4.0: Managing the digital transformation*. Springer.
Westerman, G., Tannou, M., Bonnet, D., Ferraris, P., & McAfee, A. (2012). The digital advantage: How digital leaders outperform their peers in every industry. *MIT Sloan Management and Capgemini Consulting, 2*, 2–23.
Xu, C., Wang, K., & Guo, M. (2017). Intelligent resource management in blockchain-based cloud datacenters. *IEEE Cloud Computing, 4*(6), 50–59.

4

Marketing 4.0 for SMEs in the Digital Era: A Customer-Centric Approach

4.1 The Evolution of Marketing: *Marketing to Digital Generations*

There is potential growth and value in using digital marketing aimed at millennials and other hyperaware and tech-savvy consumers. Still, marketing strategies must be perceived positively by this online generation.

Over recent years, customers' cohorts have been classified by the birth year of people composing them. Today, customers' cohorts differ more than ever based on the average age of customers, and this is a critical element that SMEs must take into consideration when designing strategies aimed at segmenting, targeting, and positioning (STP model) their products in a specific market (Camilleri, 2018). The principal factors related to these differences between customers' cohorts are linked with the different social, economic, and technical backgrounds of the people forming them (Roberts & Manolis, 2000). Obviously, someone born in the early 1950s or 1960s has grown in a postwar economic context characterized by impressive growth rates; thus, they may be a person showing greater optimism having lived in an age portrayed by tremendous opportunities

R. Rialti, L. Zollo, *Digital Transformation of SME Marketing Strategies*,
https://doi.org/10.1007/978-3-031-33646-1_4

for self-realization. Digital technologies in such times were perceived as something exclusive and not utilizable at any moment of the day. Someone born during the 1980s, instead, has probably experienced the cold war and the related political and economic unrest. However, as they may have lived in a positive economic conjecture too (the 1990s), he/she may be positive about the future anyway. Finally, anyone born in the late 1980s or early 1990s experienced both digital technology diffusion and the 2007–2012 economic downturn. Thus, someone born in the late 1980s or early 1990s will probably be quite skeptical about future possibilities. Still, he/she will probably be extremely fond of using any digital technology.

Accordingly, marketers today need to be capable of dealing with the following consumer cohorts:

1. **Baby Boomers**

Baby boomers are the people approximatively born between 1946 and 1964, representing 21.16% of the USA population (Statista, 2021). Most of them were either sons or daughters of soldiers who fought in WWII or of people who were kids or adolescents during the WWII. People from this customers' cohort were the first ones to challenge the traditional social paradigms. Baby boomers, in fact, tried to distinguish themselves from their parents by following different social rules that evolved in some cases, into specific subcultures (i.e., the hippie subculture). With respect to their parents, baby boomers were characterized by a greater openness to new technologies and different cultures. An example of the difference between baby boomers and their parents is represented by their participation in civil rights movements. Hence, baby boomers' presence in the market was the spark that lighted up the very first forms of globalization, a phenomenon that fully materialized during the age of Generation X. Regarding their consumption habits, baby boomers grew up during the 'golden age' of traditional SMEs (Roberts & Manolis, 2000). Consequently, while they are currently adopting digital technologies, they still use primarily physical stores and prefer to be assisted during their purchase experience.

2. **Generation X**

Generation X (representing 19.83% of the USA population; Statista, 2021) is formed by people born approximatively between 1965 and 1977; thus, people belonging to this cohort were adolescents or young adults during the 1980s. This cohort is widely considered more dynamic than their parents (Kumar & Lim, 2008). While the socioeconomic context during the 1980s was shaped by the end of the Cold War and a certain degree of unrest (i.e., Thatcherism, the fall of the Berlin Wall, or the demise of the Soviet Union), during this time, most of the developed countries' economies were thriving. Therefore, it emerges why this cohort was extremely optimistic about the possibility of starting new ventures (particularly in the case of such new experiences operating in the digital technologies industry). Similarly, it was the very first generation not worried about career changes, as they were—as in the case of yuppies—more career-focused than family-focused. Such a cohort was the very first to experience digital technologies (i.e., computers) during their late education. These people show a different attitude toward technologies concerning baby boomers. Specifically, they are generally not afraid of using digital technologies for purchases of products or services. They still prefer face-to-face interactions with salespersons; in fact, they are more anchored to the importance of human interaction than their younger counterparts. This phenomenon is related to the fact that the very first digital artifacts they were using were personal computers in place of mobile ones such as smartphones. Hence, they recognize the importance of digital technologies, but these technologies do not play a totalizing role in their lives.

3. **Generation Y (or Millennials)**

Generation Y includes people born roughly from 1978 to 1995, representing 21.75% of the US population (Statista, 2021) and thus being the most populated US cohort. They reached adulthood during the first and second decade of the new millennium, which is the main motivation underlying why they are also called Millennials. They grew up in the globalized economy, are prone to travel to different countries, and are naturally born freelancers (Taken Smith, 2012). They started their careers in a very turbulent economic environment characterized by frequent and abrupt downturns and sudden sharp upswings. Hence, such a cohort is usually characterized by high adaptability to change but also by pessimism about their future and their career perspectives. This notwithstanding, this cohort is currently the most technology-expert cohort among those in the market (Zollo et al., 2020). Millennials grew up with computers in their houses, internet, laptops, and mobile phones (Kumar & Lim, 2008). They were frequently very early adopters of smartphones and tablets, and they are not afraid to try new technological innovations.

In comparison with other older generations, they are highly prone to both exchanging information using digital technologies and purchasing products online. The emergence of these new customers dramatically affected traditional marketing strategies. On the one hand, it emerged that there is a need to understand how to target millennials. On the other hand, SMEs faced problems related to the new preferences of such customers to what concerned online shopping (Taken Smith & Brower, 2012).

4. Generation Z

Generation Z is formed by people born after 1996, representing 20.67% of the USA population (Statista, 2021). Most of them are just approaching the end of their education paths or are in the early stages of their professional careers. Regarding their objectives, unlike Millennials forming Generation Y, they usually try to seek stability and security (which they may potentially achieve because of current economic stability). They were raised with digital technologies. Thus, they consider any digital artifact fundamental to their lives (Turner, 2015). They are confident with any digital technologies (i.e., the digital natives or tech-savvy generation; Zollo, Rialti et al., 2022), and the increase in their spending power will cause a business model disruption even greater than that caused by the emergence of millennials. They will seek a completely digitalized purchase experience, which may cause the complete obsolescence of traditional SMEs shortly.

Among the aforementioned customers' cohorts, over recent times, millennials belonging to Generation Y have emerged as the most considered by marketing strategists and marketing researchers. The behavior of baby boomers is well known by anyone involved in marketing. Similarly, the adoption of digital technologies by Generation X does not pose significant challenges for marketing strategies, as Generation X's behavior concerning technology-enhanced marketing is still quite predictable, and this generation is indeed still behaving quite coherently to traditional consumers' behavior paradigms. For instance, while they frequently use digital platforms, they still prefer physical stores for most purchases. Finally, Generation Z spending power is still not significant enough to completely influence marketing strategies in the immediate future. Hence, the current great challenge for any marketing strategist is to unpack millennial behavior and develop strategies capable of attracting their attention.

As previously hinted, the expression millennials best describe the current grown-digital cohort of customers (Fromm & Garton, 2013). In fact, they are the very first generation composed of digital natives who usually first experience a product or a brand on digital platforms (Bergman et al., 2011). Digital technologies such as smartphones, tablets, smartwatches, and laptops are omnipresent in millennials' lives. They use any technology to accomplish most of the recurrent daily tasks; thus, such digital technologies obviously influence their effective behavior. Specifically, millennials may access websites, digital retailing platforms, and social media due to these technologies. This phenomenon is extremely important, as they may obtain extremely influential information about products they want to consider for purchase. Hence, how influencing the perceptions of such customers has become fundamental to survive in the current digital environment, and it may indeed prove useful to increase the effectiveness of communication with millennials and to foster their online purchase behavior.

Digital technologies are then fundamental to getting in touch with millennials. In any case, it is good to always remember that millennials are more mature digitally than baby boomers and Generation X. Millennials are, in fact, capable of evaluating different opportunities emerging on the internet and of critically evaluating the communication strategies of any brand or any SME. Millennials, for example, expect customized communications from brands. Millennials highly appreciate digital initiatives because they are attracted to the sensory, emotional, and intellectual stimulation that digital communication may generate (Hamzah et al., 2014). Millennials, in detail, seek three such kinds of experiences from digital platforms such as social media (Karapanos et al., 2016; Stewart et al., 2017). First, any type of communication online should be able to trigger millennial senses such as sight, hear, and touch, as this will stimulate millennials' minds and make them remember their online interaction with brands (Yoon, 2013). Second, communication should be able to trigger stimuli in millennials' cognitive sphere. To do so, online communications with millennials should be evocative and foster the remembrance of previous positive experiences. Coherently, it emerges that there is a need for marketers to know the previous experiences of customers, as it is fundamental to developing new communications (Zarantonello & Schmitt, 2010). Finally, communication with millennials needs to be characterized by being intellectually stimulating. Thus, trivial communications' times are over. In fact, communication targeting millennials should be able to stimulate customers' intellect (Verhagen et al., 2015). For example, communication strategies should be adept at making millennials crave to see a successive one from the same brand.

In addition, if marketing managers wish to target millennials, there is a need to understand that these customers tend to use digital technology hastily, impulsively, and impatiently (Stewart et al., 2017). In fact, while millennials often use social media to enhance their moods, gain product- or brand-related experiential learning (Apaolaza et al., 2014), and connect and socialize (Lien & Cao, 2014), they are also customers characterized by time-saving attitudes. Therefore, marketers should never forget that communications with millennials should not contain useless details. Millennials' attention to marketing communication may decrease in a very short time.

Building on this, it was identified that the best way to communicate with millennials may be by using social media. Social media marketing (SMM) is the best marketing communication strategy to deal with millennials and to meet their request for customized communication and their quest for sensory, emotional, and intellectual stimulation (Bergman et al., 2011; Di Benedetto & Kim, 2016). SMM is a marketing communication form based on social media enabling marketers to engage consumers in a digital conversation. Due to social media interactivity, SMM may be strategically important for targeting millennials, who usually look for customized and conspicuous experiences deriving from interactions with brands (Ko et al., 2007). SMM may respect millennial expectations of digital communication (Bergman et al., 2011; Gao & Feng, 2016; Verhagen et al., 2015). Consequently, it has been observed how SMM may allow millennials to mature loyalty toward a brand due to recurrent interactions on social media with it (Di Benedetto & Kim, 2016). This phenomenon will happen as SMM communication may reinforce millennials' perceptions associated with brands and elevate 'brand value by creating a platform to exchange ideas and information among people online' (Kim & Ko, 2012, p. 1480).

In the current environment, anyone trying to approach millennials on social media should never forget that social media may currently be used as a complementary e-commerce platform (i.e., Facebook Marketplace). Hence, marketers should never forget that SMM marketing strategies should also aim to convince millennials to purchase a product directly on social commerce platforms.

As hinted at in the first part of this section, while SMM strategies may be appropriate to target millennials, they may also have tricky and unpredictable effects if poorly executed. For example, a poor social media strategy may cause indignation in consumers, which may cause attacks from them on social media (Rialti et al., 2016). Millennials are more critical than their parents or Generation X counterparts. They are concerned about the contents of any communication and may be very disappointed by inappropriate communications (i.e., the very recent Dolce & Gabbana marketing campaign in China, which was characterized by some un explicit form of racial stereotype). Similarly, competitors may take advantage of the wrong strategies, as they may replicate new communications online to try to obtain latest market shares. The social media world is dynamic, and analytic tools to detect consumers' perceptions of implemented strategies and competitors' strategies are fundamental.

4.2 Marketing in the Digital Age and the New Customer Journey

Consumers today connect with brands in fundamentally new ways, often through media channels that are beyond SMEs' control. That means traditional marketing strategies must be redesigned coherently on how brand relationships have changed. Hence, in the digital era, brand positioning is more than ever at the heart of any solid brand strategy and should be the guiding element for shaping the experiences that customers have with their brand. This is even more important in the digital space, where the opportunity for brands and audiences to engage is at the forefront.

Traditionally, brand was identified as 'a firm-owned and controlled asset that can be built in the consumer minds through carefully coordinated marketing activities' (Gensler et al., 2013, p. 243). Hence, the brand, design, image, and positioning have traditionally been related to business-started strategies. Decisions from the business related to the wished brand positioning (i.e., cheap/expensive, high/low quality) were the only driver influencing how customers should perceive the brand. This conventional view is still dominant in brand management practices, although the understanding of what a brand is and how it should be managed is progressively changing in parallel with customers' cultural evolution, the emergence of millennials as the primary customer segment and, specifically, the diffusion of digital technologies.

The diffusion of digital technologies and the increased customers' usage of social media and online platforms exerted a huge impact on branding strategies (Rialti et al., 2016). How was it possible for digital technologies to disrupt branding strategies so significantly? Why do digital technologies (and social media) change the way managers deal with customers during branding campaigns? How many marketers exploit these new technologies? These are the questions that need to be addressed to provide a marketing manager with all the information about how to deal with branding in the digital era.

A few years ago, according to Aaker (2015, p. 37), it was extremely challenging for businesses to 'create a program that fully leverages and applies the power, the scope, and the potential synergies of the richness of the digital world. A central problem is that firms fixate on "digital" silo entity when there are many dozens of forms that digital can take'. Indeed, in the early stages of the digital revolution, businesses were not fully capable of developing integrated offline/online branding strategies. On the one hand, most of the companies were not skilled enough to integrate brand-related content generated by the business with those generated by customers. On the other hand, most of them were still not aware of the existence of most online platforms and their potentialities. Indeed, most traditional businesses were not completely conscious of the principal brand-related potentialities linked to new digital environments (e.g., brand reputation monitoring, paid search, social media advertising, or content management). In the very first years of the second decade of the new millennium, search engine management (SEM) and social media marketing (SMM) were perceived as something not truly required to outperform competitors or for survival by most businesses. It was the dawn of the digital era, so the attention toward digital technologies as branding tools was not as high as deserved.

When digital technologies started to permeate moments of customers' lives, marketers' attention toward the implications of such technologies for branding started to increase dramatically. It emerged how digital platforms such as social media and electronic marketplaces became new touchpoints between customers and businesses, enacting customers to communicate freely their opinions to a worldwide audience for the first time (Yadav & Pavlou, 2014). This was the moment in which branding strategies first included mechanisms to monitor customers' brand perceptions, brand positioning, and competitors' actions in the digital environment (Fournier & Avery, 2011). In fact, social media and any online platform allow customers to create and exchange so-called UGCs or user-generated content (Kaplan & Haenlein, 2010). UGCs may have several forms, that is, they can be shared photos on Instagram, posts on Facebook, tweets on Twitter, any kind of recension on any travel website/fare aggregator (i.e., TripAdvisor or Booking.com), or any kind of feedback on e-tailer platforms such as Amazon.com or Alibaba. As is possible to understand, UGCs may dramatically change branding strategies as we know. Specifically, due to UGCs diffused on social media and similar platforms, customers may currently influence each other's perceptions of a brand (in particular for fashionable products).

This new purchase process, which influences branding strategies directly, as we will see through this chapter, has been named by Edelman as the 'customer journey' (2010). According to the author, before digital technologies' diffusion, customers' purchase processes were based on the widely known 'funnel' paradigm—according to which customers were winnowing their purchase choices starting from many brands to progressively fewer brands until a final selection was made, such as in a funnel. Today, instead, customers are behaving in the aforementioned 'customer decision journey'. This latter framework theorizes an iterative dynamic customer decision based on five stages: awareness, consideration, purchase, retention, and advocacy (Edelman, 2010). In detail, the modern 'customer journey' begins with the consideration of a reduced set of product/service alternatives with respect to before by customers. In fact, as a consequence of stimuli from the digital environment about specific products, modern customers are already aware of offerings' possibilities in the market. In the online environment, customers are exposed to a huge number of customized advertisements; thus, they already know what the market can offer them without having to go to several physical stores to discover existing products. Then, this initial set is slowly reduced by the customer by the evaluation of other consumers' online feedback and experiences with products from the initially considered brands and alternative ones. The result is the practical purchase of a product or a service. After the purchase, the post-purchase phases start. In fact, the purchase may highly affect customer-brand relationships. After the purchase and use of a specific product from a particular brand, a customer may start to experience the products' specifications and move to a product- and brand-related experience (McAlexander et al., 2002). In the digital era, customers usually share their product- and brand-related experiences online, and in the case of satisfactory experiences, 'they'll advocate for it by word of mouth, creating fodder for the evaluations of others and invigorating a brand's potential' (Edelman, 2010, p. 3). If any problem has damaged customers' experience, they will complain by diffusing negative feedback about the product and the brand. Thus, instead of advocating for the brand, they will tarnish the brand.

Here, it emerges why the brand is no more a business-controlled asset. Currently, traditional branding strategies matter to what concern the definition of the initial positioning of the brand, but negative feedback from customers may change it abruptly and suddenly. After all, the brand's positioning is extremely related to how customers perceive the brand. Thus, if customers are provided an instrument (such as digital technologies offering the opportunity to diffuse UCGs) to self-influence each other, it emerges how customers may change the brand's positioning over time. A huge flow of negative feedback can tarnish the image of even the best-positioned brands, changing their positioning from top-quality and well-reputed brands to low-quality and not reputable ones. This phenomenon will also influence sales. UGCs in digital platforms are part of the consumers' unimaginable volume of information that a customer may access to compare different products and brands. Hence, customers' effective purchase decisions are extremely linked to how existing UGCs have changed the brand's positioning (Lemon & Verhoef, 2016). This notwithstanding, UGCs are not necessarily and univocally related to potential damage to brand image. Numerous UGCs containing positive feedback may also upgrade the positioning of a brand. Positive feedback is, in effect, valued by consumers as much as negative feedback; thus, it can positively influence the willingness to purchase a product.

To describe this new way of conducting branding, Fournier and Avery (2011) used the metaphor of 'open source' branding strategies. Similarly, more recent research has pointed out how marketing managers live in the era of 'brand cocreation' (Rialti, Caliandro et al., 2018). Indeed, according to Hatch and Schultz (2010), customers may contribute to cocreating a brand 'through network relations and social interactions among the ecosystem of all stakeholders' (p.592). Thus, scholars have evidenced how to exploit these by engaging and stimulating them to generate positive brand content to influence the most potential new consumers (Hatch & Schultz, 2010). One way to do that may be by providing incentives for customers to share UGCs online (Edelman, 2010). Similarly, brand strategists may provide 'suggestions' to consumers and pilot the contents that will be diffused. For instance, brand strategists wishing to give a particular shape to a brand may ask consumers participating in a social media brand community to share some specific kinds of content compared to another (Ramaswamy & Ozcan, 2016). Hence, consumers' shared online content may act as a powerful marketing communication tool capable of cocreating the brand.

However, brand strategists should also constantly monitor the sentiment trend of content (Flavián & Guinalíu, 2006; Rialti et al., 2016). Even when everything may seem ok in relation to UGCs, an expert marketing manager may identify the signs of a downswing in customers' perception of the brand and act promptly to change the trend (i.e., by providing honest feedback to customers or asking them why they were not satisfied). To what extent a marketing manager is able to engage customers in digital discourses and obtain their trust is fundamental. The more customers will dialog with him/her, the more problems or potentialities about the brand will be easily detected.

As it is possible to understand, SMEs operating in a digital environment should be highly aware of the functioning of the customer journey. Indeed, customers tend to generate feedback after a (online) purchase, and if such feedback is publicly shared, it may influence the positioning of SMEs and tarnish their brand.

Consumer behavior researchers have started to use psychological lenses to understand better how consumers and social media users look for 'social reassurance' when purchasing products or services online (Zollo, Carranza et al., 2021). Specifically, these authors used the widely acknowledged theory of social proof by Cialdini (1993), stating that 'keeping within one's network similar others using a product provides a sort of "social proof" that the product is worthwhile and desirable—consumers tend to decide their most appropriate behavior in a determined situation by examining others, especially "significant" and "important" others' (Zollo, Carranza et al., 2021, p. 2). Hence, we need to build on social psychology theories of influence and persuasion to deeply dive into contemporary consumers' minds and better discover how they use and experience online purchases, for example, through social media.

An example of this is a current customer's online shopping process, as illustrated in Fig. 4.1. The main underlying rationale of the model shown in Fig. 4.1 is that SMEs have to *convert* (turn, transform) a consumer—which is at first a 'stranger' toward the brand—into a lead (a person who has an initial interaction with the company) that will become a prospect

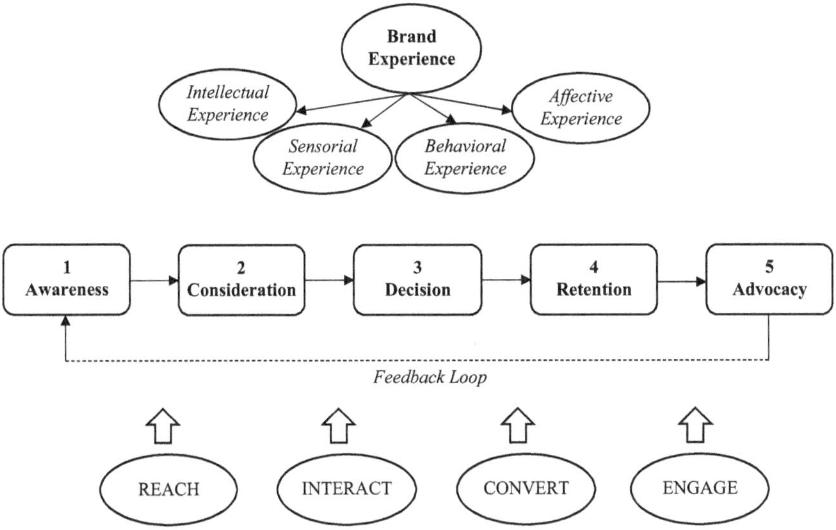

Fig. 4.1 Hypothesized conceptual model. Source: Authors' elaboration

(a consumer who shows a potential positive intention toward the brand) and, finally, a customer after the economic transaction or a strategic activities such as subscription to a freemium service.

Our framework (Fig. 4.1) consists of three main dimensions. First, the central layer illustrates the customer journey across the pre- and post-purchase phases (Lemon & Verhoef, 2016). Second, the top layer shows how this buying decision is a multidimensional process characterized by different experiential levels (Brakus et al., 2009). Finally, the bottom layer refers to the RACE model (Chaffey & Ellis-Chadwick, 2016). This step-by-step practical approach describes four important strategic acts that each SME must implement to 'walk' its customers across the journey.

The customer journey starts with the *awareness* stage, where consumers 'discover' the company's product or service that might address their needs. In this phase, it is essential that SMEs are present through a significant touchpoint to effectively interact with their *buyer persona* (i.e., the targeted customer). The main goal here is to make consumers aware that the brand can provide a unique, convenient, and tailored solution to their pain. Digital touchpoints—such as social media channels, online platforms, or virtual communities—allow brands to reach a wider audience and a greater market share than possible through physical touchpoints only. The journey continues with the *consideration* stage, where consumers assess the existing alternatives present in the offline/online market, trying to look for the best solution to their need. This is where social proof assumes the highest role: consumers seek feedback from other customers to obtain information about the desired product. In this stage, SMEs have to work on the alignment between UGC (content generated by customers about their products) and FGC (content generated by the company). Naturally, brand identity-image fitting is fundamental to this purpose. If we take the Amazon case as a benchmark, consumers usually (1) search for a product, (2) immediately jump to the reviews section, and (3) eventually add the item to the cart. This demonstrates the crucial role of having positive, verified, and reliable/credible reviews from previous customers. Then, we have the most important 'moment of truth', the final decision of the buying process journey: to purchase or not purchase the product. We know that the customer journey has a 'funnel' shape, meaning that out of several potentially interested leads, only a few become prospects intentioned to purchase, and even fewer turn into actual customers purchasing the product. Hence, it is essential that SMEs design a buying journey that is as linear, simple, and smart as possible to avoid consumers' rethinking or possibly abandoning during the process. All the touchpoints occurring during the journey must be consistently aligned with what the consumer is looking for. Even in the case of bouncing off the journey, the SME's marketers must think of a remarketing or retargeting strategy to take back their persona. Therefore the framework (Fig. 4.1) shows a backward arrow indicating a possible dynamic loop when consumers do not continue the journey linearly. Finally, one of the most important stages is the advocacy stage, where the customer him/herself becomes an endorser and ambassador of the brand by spreading positive eWOM thanks to reactions, reviews, and content aimed at stressing the positive brand experience. This leads us to the second dimension of the model, which refers to the multidimensional nature of modern brand experience.

According to Brakus et al.'s (2009) seminal work, brands have different impacts on customer experience (CX) (see also Rialti, Filieri et al., 2022).

The authors conceptualized a framework stressing how CX has four main dimensions: intellectual (at a cognitive level), behavioral, sensorial, and affective (i.e., emotional). Although it is not possible to generalize what is the brand experience dimension that most impacts a customer journey, we might hypothesize that the first stage of awareness is highly related to an intellectual experience—a consumer reflects on their need and deliberately searches for the most valuable solution. Let us take the example of a man willing to buy a ring to his wife. He will search for some general keywords on Google, for example, 'ring-gift-wife'. SMEs must work on the 'intellectual' level to *reach* (first stage of the RACE model) the customer and make him aware of their product (i.e., a beautiful gold ring perfect for a romantic present). The *discovery* phase—meaning our man realizing that a specific company has the ring he is looking for—is practical if the query of the consumer perfectly matches the keywords used by the brand to describe its products. This is where search engine optimization (SEO) usually takes place. The greater the content used by the SME is 'optimized' concerning the need and pain felt by the consumer, the higher the chances s/he will continue the journey toward the next stage, consideration.

In the second stage, our man starts *considering* many variables related to the ring alternatives he found: price, features, tone of voice, brand image, reviews, and so on. This is not only an intellectual experience—the consumer deliberately considers and evaluates the different products—but also a 'sensory' experience. Brands should be effective in building a connection (*interact* in the RACE model) with the lead able to elicit his/her senses and memory. In our example, after watching a video made by the brand on several ring options might, the man might construe a future scenario when his wife will positively react during their romantic scene. In other words, the product perfectly matches the consumer's desired situation. Companies able to pursue this goal will create what we call 'brand stickiness' (Tsai, 2014), which means positive positioning in consumers' minds or, in other words, being present as the immediate solution that comes in people's minds when thinking about a particular object—such as Tiffany's diamond ring is usually recognized as the 'quintessential expression of love[1]' for an engagement/wedding gift.

[1] See Tiffany's website: shorturl.at/gjlGN.

In this case, senses such as sight or vision are important in the online customer journey: our man will see the ring online but also self-construe a visionary scenario of himself giving a ring to his wife.

The next phase of the *decision* is mainly a 'behavioral' experience, where the consumer buys the product (the *conversion* phase in the RACE model). After the awareness and consideration stages, our man finally decides to buy a ring from a specific brand. This behavior will mark the most important touchpoint between and the company, which is why it is called the ultimate 'moment of truth' across the journey. Thanks to this action, the buying process ends, and the post-purchase process starts, where the consumer will finally have the possibility to give his gift and realize whether his decision was appropriate or not (Nosi et al., 2022). Depending on this outcome, SMEs can retain or not retain their customers: if the behavioral experience of buying the product is positive, chances are high that they will come back again for another brand's product (a new jewel for the wife); conversely, if the post-purchase is bad, the customer will likely try to forget this experience and, in the worst case for the brand, leave negative feedback and reviews. Therefore, after the purchase, the journey splits into three possible scenarios: (1) the brand experience is deemed bad, and our man leaves negative comments about the ring and the brand; (2) the experience is good, and the man leaves positive comments and eWOM, thus becoming a brand advocate/ambassador; and (3) the customer does not leave any reaction, so it is not possible to retrieve information about his behavior post-purchase. Building on these scenarios (negative, positive, neutral), brands will take different actions, such as communicating with the customer to understand why the purchase experience went wrong; interact with the customer to incentivize them to buy a new product of the same brand; remarket the customer to better know how the shopping experience (CX analysis) was and gather feedback. In any case, emotions and feelings strongly impact the post-purchase stage, which is why it is generally understood as an 'affective' experience. Being able to generate positive emotions in the post-purchase stage requires the ability to *engage* (final action of the RACE model) customers, for example, in the brand community, to create a feeling of belongingness with the brand's world. In our example, if the wife will positively react to gift-giving (showing feelings of happiness, joy, surprise, love, etc.), it is likely that our man will share his positive brand experience with his significant others and even recommend the brand for that product.

4.3 Big Data for Big Profit

Among the most disrupting elements characterizing the 4.0 Era, big data and the tools and procedures to analyze them have been the most discussed ones by managerial literature. While sometimes regarded as information only available to large businesses, it is necessary to consider how they are currently available even for SMEs (Troise et al., 2022). The intersection of data obtainable from online sources and those derived from legacy systems may generate huge amounts of data frequently neglected by SMEs (Kim & Moon, 2021). Aside from the consideration of new touchpoints (which are anyway data sources too), implementing tools to collect and analyze big data is what changed marketing strategies in SMEs at most. Thanks to big data, these businesses may obtain more information than ever about customers. Such information could be extremely useful in the management of customer decision-making cycles, as well as in managing customers' lifetime cycles (Troise et al., 2022).

Big data have radically affected traditional ways of running a business (McAfee & Brynjolfsson, 2012). Today, due to big data, managers have large amounts of information at their disposal and, consequently, are increasingly informed about the state of internal operations, the efficiency of supply chain processes, the workforce's performance, and customers' behavior (Erevelles et al., 2016). As it is possible to imagine, decision-making processes have simultaneously evolved. Managers, as such, can decide upon the most suitable strategy to implement according to this newly available information. Accordingly, McAfee and Brynjolfsson observed how 'smart leaders across industries will see using big data for what it is: a management revolution' (2012, p. 5). Information has, in fact, always been identified as one of the most important value-creating factors for any organization; however, big data have brought information value creation potential to a whole new level.

Big data differs from traditional large datasets in volume, velocity, variety, veracity, value, variability, and visualization—or the 'Seven Vs of Big Data' (Mishra et al., 2017). Among these seven Vs, the original four were recognized in IBM's seminal document on big data (www.ibm.com), and the other three Vs were later identified by scholars in successive years. Anyway, what does each V mean?

i. **Volume**

Volume refers to the sheer dimensions of this typology of datasets (McAfee & Brynjolfsson, 2012). Contemporary large organizations are, in fact, capable of collecting vast quantities of data in a very short time (Rialti, Caliandro et al., 2018), meaning that big data dataset dimensions frequently exceed the terabyte (Mishra et al., 2017). This phenomenon is quite easy to understand in the current digital environment. For instance, Facebook has more active users than the whole population of China. Consequently, think about the size of its datasets collecting all the data about users' interactions and UGCs. Otherwise, a very good example of the size of big data derives from the fact that currently, most businesses rely on the IoT, which provides for generating a huge quantity of data by sensors embedded in machines.

ii. **Velocity**

The velocity of big data is the 'rate at which data are generated and the speed at which it should be analyzed and acted upon' (Gandomi & Haider, 2015, p. 138). Specifically, in the big data era, data are constantly generated by any device connected to the internet. Businesses should be able to grasp, process, and activate big data at any moment without interruption (Wamba et al., 2015). Indeed, as data are generated from users' and machines' interactions in digital environments, their generation occurs over time. Thus, an extensive data dataset's dimension may increase with incredible speed in a matter of a few seconds. This can be represented by Alibaba Black Friday's case. For most of the day, more than 10,000 transactions were registered every second on Alibaba's ledgers.

iii. **Variety**

Building on the previous assumption that any device connected to the internet may be the source of big data, it is possible to understand the meaning of the next V—big data's variety. Variety in a big data context is related to the 'heterogeneous sources of big data (i.e., sensors embedded in machines, customers' activities on social media, B2C or B2B digital interactions, etc.) and the consequent heterogeneous formats that the files composing big data may assume' (Rialti, Marzi et al., 2018, p. 7). Indeed, several different types of files may compose big data, that is, photographs, sensor data, tweets, and encrypted packets. As is visible, these typologies of data cannot be represented using the old row and column databases. Big data components are indeed making them unstructured. This means it will be impossible to fit them on a spreadsheet or a database application with the right analytic techniques.

iv. **Veracity**

Veracity is related to the necessary degree of trustworthiness that big data sources must possess (Mishra et al., 2017). Indeed, online environments are densely populated by fake news, unreliable sources, and untrustworthy information providers. Hence, why internally collected data are essential emerges. Internal data, in fact, come from identifiable quality sources.

v. **Value**

Value is linked to the economic value generated by an organization's processes and technologies that analyze big data (Yin & Kaynak, 2015). In fact, information may be considered a fundamental productive factor and a source of competitive advantages. Some information, that is, information about our customer base or information about competition may allow a business to be more competitive. Thus, big data may enable modern businesses to create value.

vi. **Variability**

Variability refers to the possible variations in data flow rate, processing, and data sources (Wamba & Mishra, 2017). Data fluxes, in fact, may reach the organization at a different pace, may require other times to be stored, and may need different times to be analyzed. Thus, variability of all characteristics and requirements over time may be a trait of an extensive data dataset.

vii. **Visualization**

Visualization concerns the possibility for data analysts to obtain visual insights as an output of extensive data analysis (Mishra et al., 2017). Indeed, if the results of data analysis are not observable, managers may not be capable of analyzing them.

Some other Vs were tentatively added over the last five years. While pertinent literature has not confirmed these variables, they are in everyday use in practice-based literature.

Among them, the most relevant are as follows:

viii. **Validity**

Validity relates to veracity. It pertains to the accuracy and correctness of data about their intended use. Research shows how approximately 60% of a data scientist's time is used to clean data before real usage (Rialti et al., 2017). Hence, a dataset could only be classified as big data when the underlying sources, such as metadata, ensure data quality and common definitions.

ix. **Vulnerability**

Vulnerability represents one of the weak points of big data. Vulnerability means that data storage systems may suffer from data leaks due to their sheer size. Additionally, as part of big data is composed of so-called open data (which may be obtained through semantic web or web crawlers), if these data are removed from online available databases, each data scientist is at risk of missing some important pieces for triangulation.

x. **Volatility**

Volatility concerns the possibility for data to be enriched over time (and the risk of becoming obsolete quickly). In detail, it refers to the rate of change in data structure and their possible lifetime. Data such as social network sentiment are highly volatile, while data from weather or social forecasts are less volatile. Understanding this trait is fundamental for businesses because it influences the usability of data themselves.

Like any business with several customers, even SMEs may benefit from big data. Indeed, this amount of detailed information about customers may have several effects. First, businesses may know customers' preferences either by looking at their online searches or by looking at their in-store behavior. In the first case, the company may collect data from its own e-commerce page, other e-commerce platforms, search engines, or social media (Erevelles et al., 2016). Using such data, information about customers' preferences or preferred products may quickly emerge. Specifically, it may be possible to identify future trends before they even materialize. In the second case, data from the use of in-store digital technologies may provide information about habitual shopping. Thus, SME managers should potentially provide suggestions about internal paths that customers should follow to reduce the time of their visits (if customers are time conscious) or provide customers with personalized promotions, which may trigger their purchases (Santoro et al., 2018).

Second, using the same kinds of data, businesses may evaluate customers' perceptions about their visit to the store or the overall purchase experience. Customers usually tend to diffuse UGCs about their visits (i.e., Facebook posts concerning a satisfactory or dissatisfactory understanding, recensions about product availability). Due to such information, a business may identify eventual downturns in customers' perception and satisfaction, both about their in-store visit and online purchase. Thus, managers may take corrective actions to influence customers' perceptions (i.e., by reducing the source of customers' unsatisfactory experience) and then increase their loyalty.

Third, SMEs may use information from big data to increase their revenues. In fact, using this information, they could potentially decide and manage which product should be in store, which should be priced differently, and which should be promoted differently. In detail, about product availability, big data has two effects. On the one hand, due to big data, a business may know which product is ending and replenish the stock. On the other hand, using big data may potentially identify, with extreme precision, the number of items that will be sold over a day, thus reducing stocks.

Regarding pricing, data about customer purchases (and consequently their sensitivity to different prices) may become more detailed than ever; thus, a business may decide the best price to maximize revenues. Customer segmentation based on prices could also be performed. Finally, as big data may contain information about the visualizations of a message, a business may also decide which channel is most suitable to promote a product (Davenport et al., 2012).

Examples of large companies' use of big data have been quite evident in recent years. Tesco, for instance, used big data to understand how customers shop for each product. Due to big data analytics and clustering techniques, Tesco's managers found how products' purchases hung together. Consequently, using these new insights, the company could order products in the store correctly. Similarly, as it was possible to know better than ever, the quantity of products that customers will purchase improved the in-store availability while reducing wastage. A similar use of big data was made by Walmart. Such data were integrated into an app by Walmart, which was made available for customers to download on their smartphones. From this perspective, because of big data, customers can now benefit from customized promotions related to the product they have to purchase in a short time.

Many SMEs still think that big data is something for big businesses. However, as we will show in the final cases, foreshadowing SMEs have found the use of big data to be fundamental to improving the performance of their operations and marketing campaigns. Manufacturing emerged as leaner thanks to big data generated by machines and employees through their smartphones and tablets. Just a bunch of sensors and actuators on production machines may generate several gigabytes of data over the years, which could be enriched by any other data in the business to create a big data dataset. Likewise, aggregated consumer data have proven fundamental for some SMEs to better identify the microtrends underlying consumer preferences. It allowed us to detect emerging markets and understand how to target them.

Moving from these considerations, big data can generate large profits in any sector and in any business, including SMEs. However, as big data are complex and unstructured, to obtain these profits, analytics techniques are necessary. Indeed, only with analytics techniques will it be possible to transform big data into small data, usable knowledge, and profits.

4.4 Transforming Big Data Into Small Data

4.4.1 Big Data, Small Data, and Smart Insights

With the right techniques, it will be possible for any business to reap the benefits of big data. In fact, without ad hoc architectures and capabilities, even if the collection and storage of big data may represent a problem, one can only imagine what kinds of issues may then arise related to the analysis of such databases.

Indeed, SMEs can face significant challenges during the process of big data analytics due to the differences between big data and traditional datasets. As assessed, it emerged how going 4.0 requires a complete change of mindset in SMEs. Coherently, the first focus point for modern SMEs should be the development of so-called big data architectures. They include networks composed of several processors, machines, and databases that can collect, processing, storing, and analyzing big data. As an example, data lakes should be the basis of these architectures. In simple terms, a data lake is a system or repository of data that is being stored in the original format. A data lake is usually a single store of all enterprise data, including raw copies of source system data and transformed data derived from sensor monitoring machines or internal processes (Gupta et al., 2018). Similarly, SMEs may need to rely on nested computer networks capable of simultaneously processing different kinds of data based on other open-source software. These networks are also capable of parallel computing and are adept in ensuring interorganizational operability to collect, categorize, store, and analyze data stored in repositories (Labrinidis & Jagadish, 2012). Most importantly, these architectures should not become a burden for organizations. Hence, they should either be capable of being adapted to evolving data or being capable of changing business structures (Rialti et al., 2019).

However, architectures alone are not sufficient. SMEs should also invest resources in personnel selection and training (Wamba & Mishra, 2017). For instance, to successfully manage data or architectures, big data analysts, scientists, and engineers need to be skilled in R, Python, Hadoop, Not Only SQL (NoSQL) data models, schema-less data retrieval, and other tools based on artificial intelligence paradigms. However, only the retraining of personnel is not sufficient, and 'big data culture' paradigms should be the basis for transforming the whole culture (Tallon & Pinsonneault, 2011). As a result, there needs to be a broader orientation toward data-driven decision making within the SME. Additionally, while making business-related decisions, employees should not be afraid to rely exclusively, or almost exclusively, on machines and data (Rialti, Caliandro et al., 2018).

Therefore, managers should be able to base their decisions on the new insights emerging from data, which should help them to make fast and smart decisions. In addition, they should be capable of deciding about the technical solutions that the organization should implement. Therefore, they should be knowledgeable enough about BDA to be capable of proposing possible technical solutions (Akter et al., 2016).

Moving from these three main requirements, the concept of BDA capabilities emerged, an ensemble of capabilities related to the 'ability to mobilize and deploy BDA-based resources in combination or co-present with other resources and capabilities'. These capabilities are directly derived from BDA personnel and management capabilities and BDA infrastructure flexibility (Wamba & Mishra, 2017, pp. 357).

According to pertinent studies, these BDA capabilities may generate competitive advantages for any business, including SMEs. Competitive advantage can be created by the information derived from big data (McAfee & Brynjolfsson, 2012). However, why will developing such capabilities generate a competitive advantage for a modern business?

Information derived from big data may ensure the necessary data flow to better support decisions. This notwithstanding, managers or decision makers need to have aggregated data along with detailed data about a phenomenon at their disposal. In such cases, the importance of small data emerges.

Small data, specifically, are a typology of data that may be derived from the partitioning of a big data dataset into more minor and more useful insights (Chen et al., 2016). From this perspective, small data are related to BDA capabilities. To identify the most useful insights from a big data dataset, such capabilities are necessary. They are also crucial so that the information can reach the correct manager at the right time. To make appropriate decisions, managers need to have only the specific information that could allow them to identify new patterns and any new information at their disposal. In fact, they do not need an overflow of information but only the specific information that may be used to create value. Certain information should have more priority, such as information about potential emerging trends, potential new customers, and potential competitive actions undertaken by competitors. Coherently, managers should not obtain such information in an unstructured form, but it should reach them in a format such as easily readable documents that contain only the fundamental points.

Therefore, using BDA capabilities, big data should be transformed into small data. These small data should also be converted into documents capable of providing managers with smart insights. This may help the manager make better, faster, and more efficient decisions, as he/she will have smart insights about a topic of particular interest.

4.4.2 Which Data Should SMEs Capture?

The possibility of obtaining insight from big data is only worthwhile if managers can drive people who should deal with data extraction toward the identification of the effectively required data.

Accordingly, if a data scientist has not been properly trained to extract the correct data, he/she will not be capable of separating what is needed from what is not applicable.

From this perspective, it is fundamental to focus on which data may help SME managers make smart decisions in the big data era.

Data about customers are a must. Customers are the only stakeholders capable of increasing revenues for any SME; hence, it is given why their data are more precious than data from anyone else. Data about their purchase habits and trends is full of meaningful information for anyone involved in decision making. Among customers' data, some are more important than others. Specifically, data about declining trends and emerging opportunities matter more than others. A manager knowing which kind of product is not appreciated by a customer may decide to stop selling that item.

Similarly, if the data contain information about the cause of such a declining trend (i.e., price, product's characteristics, obsolescence of the product), such a manager may act promptly to solve the problem itself (i.e., by changing the price). Data containing insights about future trends may be used to decide which product could be sold in the future (Erevelles et al., 2016). Specifically, such data may help decide which product to commercialize among several different opportunities. Finally, data about customers may help in the identification of new niches that may be targeted because of new marketing campaigns (Couldry & Turow, 2014). Likewise, data about customers' in-store experience and customers' loyalty are fundamental. If it may emerge that customers' experience is sharply decreasing, a manager may decide to modify the store atmosphere and environment to prevent customers from switching their loyalty toward a competitor.

Data about competitors are as relevant as customer data. In detail, due to big data analytics, it may be possible to identify competitors' strategies and why customers prefer their stores over ours. Online environments such as social media may contain information about who is being targeted by a competitor or the new products it is attempting to launch. Information about its prices may also be easily identified in a very short time by collecting data from its platforms. Accordingly, a manager may decide more accurately when it will be the moment to start a price war or which customer segment may be more profitable and decide which new strategy is more suitable to survive.

Another typology of useful data is advertising channel effectiveness. Using big data analytics, a highly detailed level of information about how much customers have visualized and advertising messages on a digital channel will be easily monitorable. BDA analytics can, in fact, make it possible to obtain information about who, when, and where one or more messages are visualized and appreciated (i.e., by observing social media metrics). In addition, it may also be possible to monitor the contents of UGCs concerning a company and its products, thus identifying what is ok and what is wrong, both with the message and with the product. Similarly, such data may also help in strategies concerning the choice of communication channel.

Finally, data about internal operations' efficiency may emerge. In fact, data about shelf replenishment percentage and the time required for a product to go from a deposit to the shelf may be better observed and reduced. Similarly, data about defective products may prove to be extremely useful. This way, corrective actions concerning reverse supply chain may be taken. Finally, data about customers' preferred payment methods could emerge.

4.4.3 The Promises and Perils of Blockchain Protocols to Analyze Big Data

The collection and analysis of big data may be both a costly and time-consuming process. The implementation of technologies to collect and analyze big data could have extremely high costs for any business. Similarly, the collection and analysis of big data may require time and sometimes may also generate unexpected expenses related to the source of data.

From this perspective, it was widely observed how very frequently SMEs may be unable to afford BDA technologies. In fact, while they may benefit from the information available online, they need help to afford both the technologies themselves and people capable of analyzing data.

Recently, some solutions for SMEs have also emerged. Among these solutions (i.e., cloud computing), blockchain has received most of the attention. Anyway, will blockchain be able to meet the promises? Similarly, what are the perils of relying exclusively on blockchain?

As previously assessed, blockchain traces its origin in the world of finance. The first use of blockchain was, in fact, as a ledger to register bitcoins' transactions. However, more recently, blockchain started to diffuse as a technology capable of helping SMEs trace transactions with customers (Karafiloski & Mishev, 2017). For instance, the Chinese full e-tailer Alibaba pioneers the use of blockchain to trace customers' purchases and payments. Any time a product is switching its ownership the transaction creates a new node, which also includes details about payments. Thus, blockchain could allow a retailer/e-tailer to monitor all the transactions occurring in its products. Similarly, costs could also be traced, thus immediately identifying which customers usually pay for a good or a service or not. However, Alibaba's blockchain applications are related to customers' transactions and relationships with suppliers. In detail, due to blockchain, large e-tailers are tracking the products they are selling from their origin, thus reducing the risk of selling counterfeited products. Indeed, if suppliers adopt blockchain protocols, they could transmit the information about everyone that managed the development to the company, thus allowing managers and marketers to know where it was produced and all the steps that brought the product to the online platform. In this way, by simply monitoring all the chains, it is possible for an SME to control and monitor all the data at its disposal.

Notwithstanding this potential of blockchain, Alibaba is one of the world's largest e-tailers/retailers; thus, it was not concerned with either the costs of blockchain development or big data analytics. In any case, could blockchain also hold some opportunities for SMEs?

The answer to this question is yes. Using blockchain protocols may allow an SME (in particular, if it is a smaller scale retailer) to better collect data from all the participants in the blockchain. In order for this to be possible, such a retailer will need to be a participant in the blockchain itself; otherwise, data will not be accessible. Indeed, data created by all the participants of the blockchain are freely accessible to everyone participating in the blockchain. Thus, blockchain is an extremely useful way for smaller retailers to collect online data. In addition, we must consider that data extracted from a blockchain could provide information about how a product is transacted between several parties, the fluxes of money and the timings and locations of purchases. Blockchain could also be essential, not only for data collection but also for big data storage and analysis.

On the one hand, each node of a blockchain could represent a point of storage of data for any small retailer wishing to save money on internal storage systems. Specifically, a small retailer could access a blockchain ledger, deposit data, and be safe that such data could not be accessed without proper authorization. One of the characteristics of blockchain protocols is privacy about stored data. Second, many blockchain providers have started to integrate machine learning and artificial intelligence as part of node generation processes with marketing, auditing, trend forecasting, and many other applications. Such providers believe that by utilizing blockchain technology, they can act in a similar fashion to big data analytics giants. Retailers can ask the provider to analyze each time they deposit the data and observe changes over time, thereby identifying trend changes. In addition, retailers can eventually track the performance of their data and usage of said data by other people. The inherent openness and honesty of the network should offer a new level of trust and transparency.

From this perspective, it is possible that due to blockchain, even smaller retailers that could not afford to implement BDA technologies or to develop BDA capabilities could exploit the potential of big data information.

Risks are present either way. In fact, on the one hand, data security breaches could occur if the ledger owner is exploiting deposited data on its own. Second, even to using blockchain, smaller retailers will need systems to share data. Finally, the use of blockchain involves very high energetic costs.

4.5 Emerging Mechanisms to Generate Competitive Advantage in the Digital Era

4.5.1 Adopting Competitive Intelligence Tools

Your competitors are already spying on you. How are you going to fight back in an ever-increasing competitive space? As the digital world continues to be complex and murky, you need tools that help you find transparency within the landscape.

Digital environments are characterized by highly high competition levels. Digital environments (such as social media, e-commerce platforms, or blogs) are indeed accessible with meager investments to anyone wishing to promote a product or a service. The emergence of a freely accessible online platform may also allow competitors to damage both the business and its market share. In fact, over recent times, it has widely been observed how a business may use social media to attack a competitor or exploit a competitor's weakness. However, social media may also allow a business and its competitors to know each other better than ever. This derives from the possibility of obtaining social media metrics concerning interactions between any business and its customers (Dishman & Calof, 2008). Hence, your business' strategy is no more a hidden gem that no one can monitor until it is effectively implemented. Still, it is something that an expert or a competitor may understand in very short time by observing social media or internet metrics. For example, if your business is trying to expand in an Asian market, a competitor may know it earlier than ever by observing the trend of internet advertisings targeting Asia and coming from your business.

Accordingly, it emerged that businesses need to implement their own competitive intelligence tools (Wright & Calof, 2006). First, they are, in fact, fundamental to identifying customers' behavior. Second, they may be helpful in decoding competitors' strategies and planning competitive reactions. Next, they are also useful to evaluate whether a competitor is spying on you or not, for example, by using interaction metrics (Crane, 2005).

From this perspective, competitive intelligence tools could be identified as the ensemble of tools that a business may use to identify digital strategies' strength, the main challenges related to the exploitation of digital channels, opportunities for future growth, and windows to increase market share (Søilen, 2017). Digital competitive intelligence tools should therefore be able to collect and interpret online data from customers and competitors. For example, digital competitive intelligence tools should collect all customers' feedback on online platforms to understand how customers perceive products, marketing strategies, and the online marketplace itself. In fact, the analysis of customer-generated content is fundamental to decodifying future market trends and identifying whether their loyalty to our business is decreasing or increasing. Advanced competitive intelligence tools may also be capable of segmenting our customers and forecasting which ones will purchase a product from our business in the future (Chen et al., 2012). Similarly, competitive intelligence tools should be capable of collecting competitors' data. In detail, first, they should be able to detect how competitors behave in the competitive arena. Then, competitive intelligence tools should collect all the possible information about competitors' digital strategies and transform these strategies into patterns, data, and graphs. Indeed, these tools should have the potential to collect information about what rivals are doing, which markets they are targeting and how customers respond to competitors' strategies (Kimble & Milolidakis, 2015). As is easily understandable, if such systems can accomplish their tasks, they may dramatically help the business to develop competitive responses. Specifically, due to such tools, a company may avoid implementing strategies that are already proven unsuccessful for competitors or identify markets that are not targeted by them. In addition, such tools should be able to detect competitors' interactions with business online content. The possibility of identifying who is visualizing your content, exploring, and sharing them represents a huge potential advantage for businesses. In fact, it will allow you to know who is spying on you, who is trying to tarnish your strategies, and how to counterattack. Indeed, your competitors are already spying on you, so you should try to implement tools to counterattack.

To do so, such tools need to be properly developed and implemented from scratch. As they are essential for businesses' competitiveness, managers should be aware of which characteristics are fundamental so that they work properly. Accordingly, four main factors are crucial. Specifically, such systems should be (1) based on proven technologies and prone to be scalable, (2) objective-based, (3) endowed with their own 'intelligence', and (4) customizable (www.bigdata-madesimple.com).

1. **The Importance of Competitive Intelligence Tools That Are Based on Proven Technologies and Scalable**

It was observed that competitive intelligence tools should be built on proven analytics technologies. Technologies such as Google Analytics

(GA), Facebook Analytics, or Amazon Web Services (AWS) are effective platforms for your business to build on a competitive intelligence tool. Such technologies are, in fact, extremely reliable (the providers mentioned above are indeed providing constant updates and support to users), usable, even to inexperienced users, and flexible in terms of potential uses. Additionally, tools based on such technologies are scalable and adaptable. Such systems are capable of being improved time by time and being usable for solving a plethora of different digital-related problems (Prilop et al., 2013).

2. The Importance of Possessing Objective-Based Tools for Competitive Intelligence

Managers should always pay attention to implementing only objective-based competitive intelligence tools. Suppose managers need to understand trends in customers. In that case, tools are necessary that can crawl data from an online environment, to analyze the content of these data, explore the trends in customer sentiment, monitor the direction of purchases, and to summarize such information into dialysable insights. Otherwise, if the scope of the system is to monitor competitors' actions, tools able to measure customers' interactions with competitors' online pages will become necessary. Indeed, only such tools may allow managers to understand which market competitors are targeting, which customers' segments, and whether competitors' contents are appreciated by customers (www.scaleoutsoftware.com).

Digital marketing analytics provide several metrics and critical indicators that were absent before this online marketing revolution. Depending on the stage of the customer journey, many online metrics might be used by digital marketers to better understand and explore their customers' social behavior (Fu et al., 2020), to gather as much information as possible to convert the targeted buyer persona. Following the GA template, the online social behavior of users might be classified into four main categories: *audience*, *acquisition*, *behavior*, and *conversion*.

Audience analysis allows SME marketers to know the socio-psycho-demographics of visitors to their website, social media, or whatever online presence platform they are using—for example, we might know the visitors' language, location, browser, operating system, mobile devices, and channels used to reach the website. Metrics such as returning users versus new users, number of sessions and session duration, page views, and bounce rate clearly depict the way users are experiencing the online presence of the company, allowing an easy understanding of the success of their digital marketing strategies (i.e., pay-per-click, SEO, traffic, and volume trade-off, and so on). Hence, this first report, named *audience*, plays a vital role in the profiling strategy of marketers, which will be able to better define the main features of their targeted audience.

The second report is labeled *acquisition* and refers to how companies attract—after reaching—their audience to their online presence. Four options are frequently used: *direct*, *paid search*, *organic search*, and *affiliates*. *Direct* means customers already know the brand name; thus, they directly type into a search engine or the browser the name of the brand they are looking for (i.e., 'Tyffany's'). In this case, the company has already gained a brand reputation and is able to directly attract their buying persona with no intermediaries or need to pay for being displayed at the top of SERPs (search engine result pages). For example, the demo account of GA related to Google Merchandise Store (the website selling Google's products and merchandise) has in the last year (December 2021–December 2022) an 84.5% direct channel, meaning that 589.265 visitors out of a total of 691.916 directly reached the website (i.e., directly typing 'Google Merchandise Store' on the search engine or browser). *Paid search*, instead, relates to paid ads that a company did to appear at the top of SERPs when users type a specific key phrase or keywords. In our example, it could be that when a user looks for 'Google merchandise' or 'Google apparel', a sponsored ad will appear at the top of the result page. In the case of Google Merchandise Store, paid search represents 10.9% in the last year (i.e., 75.765 visitors out of 691.916 used a paid search channel to visit the Google Store). The paid search strategy is crucial for new companies or SMEs attempting to gain higher positions in the targeted SERP, but incumbents also use this strategy to appear in the top section of the results. *Organic search* is a term usually referred to as SEO, meaning that without the need to pay anything, the company's website, products, or services appear in the SERP in the non-advertised section. This is one of the best accomplishments for digital marketers because, thanks to a perfect optimization of the content, communication, and keywords used in their online presence, users' queries will match the brand's website or social media profile. It is also very difficult, as demonstrated by the GA report of Google Merchandise Store, that scores less than 1% in terms of organic search in the last year. Finally, affiliate *marketing* refers to building and strengthening partnerships with stakeholders' websites to receive backlinks from such affiliates' online presence. Depending on the affiliated partner, this strategy might be expensive, but for sure, it will increase the authority of our website and online presence if designed in a coherent and consistent way concerning the mission and vision of the company (in other words, avoiding blackhat techniques).

The third report shown in GA is *behavior*, which relates to the most engaging site content as perceived by the visitor, the site speed (page and user timings, which are among the most impacting core web vitals to be monitored), and the 'behavior flow', which indicates the number of interactions a visitor had across the journey using a funnel approach—that is, after visiting the landing page, how many visitors continue the path toward the starting pages, then the first interaction with a call-to-action, then the second interaction, and so on and so forth, until the final goal: conversion from lead to prospect, and in turn from possibility to customer. Using the Google Merchandise Store example, well exemplifies how retaining visitors across the digital journey is difficult: out of 459,000 home visits, 83,000 visitors had a first interaction, and 55,000 had a second interaction with the website. One of the goals of digital marketers is to reduce these drop-offs, which indicates a nonengaging experience during website visits. The greater the buyer persona's online behavior is investigated, the better the content and personalized experience the company will be able to provide. This is one of the most important sources of success and competitive advantage in modern digital marketing.

Finally, *conversions* are the quintessential indicator for digital marketers. As stated in this book, the main goal for SMEs trying to translate their presence in online and social environments is to convert a visitor of their website or social media profile into a customer. Call-to-actions are essential because they allow interactive communication and bidirectionality among the consumer/customer and the brand. GA indicates the online 'location' where conversions typically take place in sections such as register, leave info, store, add to basket, sign in, leave feedback, and so on. The greater the company can interact and dynamically engage the targeted audience, the higher the probability of conversions. Digital marketers are not satisfied with high traffic, volume, visits, or returning visitors to their website if these behaviors do not lead to the main final goal: conversion.

3. **The Importance of Artificial Intelligence for Competitive Intelligence Tools**

Competitive intelligence tools need to be able to prioritize information on their own. Thus, it emerges how such systems need to be endowed with a form of 'intelligence'. Accordingly, they should work according to artificial intelligence paradigms, such as machine learning. Indeed, if the tool can learn on its own which information should have priority, it will be able to provide more meaningful information to the users (Jourdan et al., 2008). In addition, competitive intelligence tools embedded with artificial intelligence capabilities (or any capability to decide on their own) may autonomously decide which content to promote or which to remove.

4. **Will Customizability Matter in Competitive Intelligence Tool Selection?**

Finally, managers should always select competitive intelligence tools that may be customized according to the specific business case and to users' capabilities. In this sense, they should be able to incorporate existing best practices without replacing them and should be able to generate the same insights that the user may require. Hence, they should not only be based on reliable technologies, scalable, objective-based, and embedded with artificial intelligence; they should also be customizable to the specific business. In fact, if a technological tool cannot be adapted to how the business is run, its employees may reject it.

If successfully implemented, the functions of such tools may be fundamental to driving digital transformation. Competitive intelligence tools are strategic tools to evaluate the way search engine optimization (SEO), mobile marketing, or social media marketing are proceeding. Specifically, they may gather insights from the web and transform them into metrics utilizable to amend marketing strategies. Such information may be used to identify whether a process is proceeding correctly or not (Rialti, Caliandro et al., 2018).

Regarding electronic commerce (e-commerce), competitive intelligence tools matter as much as digital marketing strategies. Competitive intelligence tools are essential to collect information about sales trends, including the market share of competitors. In the digital era, information is what matters most when implementing strategies aimed at increasing sales. Hence, the role of such tools is more evident than ever. Indeed, because of competitive intelligence tools, it is possible to detect what customers want. Accordingly, businesses may identify the right value proposition and the best business model to develop.

4.5.2 Adapting the Value Proposition

In the digital era, as previously assessed, it also emerged how digital products are progressively becoming complementary to physical products. A very well-known example can be represented by a customer who has purchased an iPhone and then purchases digital music on iTunes (here, digital music is complementary to the physical iPhone). In the current times, therefore, it is unthinkable for a customer to purchase a laptop without ever having considered that sooner or later, he/she will need to purchase additional software. Similarly, younger customers are increasingly interested in the possibility of customizing the products or the product baskets they will buy. It is then emerging how any SME needs to rethink its value proposition. From this perspective, SMEs may follow three ways to transform their value proposition:

Offering of Digital Products in Addition to Physical Ones

The first way is the sale as mentioned above of digital goods to customers. Specifically, SME retailers (or at least one of their business units acting as an electronic retailer, a.k.a. e-tailer) could decide to start selling digital products complementary to physical ones. Sometimes, such digital products may generate more profit than physical products. It is not infrequent that some computer software, smartphone applications, or digital products such as e-books/digital music/videogames are cash cows for many businesses, while physical products are sold underpriced just to enable customers to purchase and use digital products. Digital products, in fact, usually generate higher margins, as they have lower (or almost none) production costs and meager distribution costs and are promoted almost exclusively via digital channels (Johnson et al., 2008). This was the case for Apple during the late years of the previous decade. The business generated high profits from selling digital music as a complementary digital product usable on Apple's iPhone. Currently, instead of retaking the example of Apple, one of the most margin-generating activities is selling Apps on the App Store. Similarly, it is possible to observe how Amazon generates a high percentage of its profits from Amazon Prime Video, its film streaming platform (Wayne, 2018).

The emergence of the Metaverse and Virtual Worlds has exacerbated the modes through which companies, including SMEs, may sell digital products. One of the main revolutions digitalization has brought to the consumer services industry is a new way of approaching property ownership through NFT, nonfungible tokens (Hofstetter et al., 2022). According to Investopedia, NFTs are crypto assets on a blockchain with unique identification codes and metadata able to distinguish these assets from others (Thampanya et al., 2020). In other words, NFTs are smart contracts written on blockchains that transfer the ownership of a specific digital asset to a consumer that bought it. For example, suppose a consumer wants to buy the ownership of a wearable digital asset (i.e., a digital version of a fashion dress designed by a luxury brand). In that case, NFTs might represent the smart contract through which the consumer will become the unique owner of that specific asset (Chohan & Paschen, 2021). Cryptocurrencies such as ether (ETH) represent the currency used to fulfill such digital transactions. A fundamental element of NFTs is that either the owner possesses the digital wearable to assess (the digital version of the fashion dress) or s/he possesses the physical version of the fashion dress, meaning that the simultaneous existence of both digital and physical versions is impossible. As a result, 'phygital' approaches are becoming increasingly common in digital environments. For example, it is pretty common currently to see brands entering metaverse platforms (such as videogames such as Fortnite, Roblox, Animal Crossing, etc.) and showcasing worldwide a digital version of their new line of dresses, and only after selling the physical capsule available in the 'real' world. This is interesting from a strategic branding perspective because it allows brands to first reach the targeted audience's attention through the metaverse platforms (i.e., the videogame), assess the reaction, and then make the proper adjustments to come out with the physical capsule.

Offering New Additional Services That Could Be Purchased Only Through an Online Platform

Another way to reap additional profits from sales on digital platforms is represented by the possibility of selling customers other services. Due to online media, customers may not only select which product to purchase but also purchase additional services such as insurance, faster delivery options, or training courses (Kim & Stoel, 2004). Customers are paying for such services; as such, the possibility of offering customers these services may increase revenues. The sale of services is highly profitable. Indeed, such services are frequently provided by third-party service providers and not the seller itself, but the seller may obtain a share of the profit from such a third party (Marcussen, 1999).

Additionally, in this case, the customer is selecting which service to purchase (while in the physical world, it was often the company deciding which additional service offer); thus, customers themselves may choose how to customize their purchase experience. This is the case for many businesses selling hi-tech products online. It is quite probable that a customer may decide to purchase integrative theft insurance or maintenance insurance if they perceive that they may get their goods stolen or that any maintenance on the product could have very high costs. For example, almost anyone purchasing a high-end smartphone (such as an iPhone or a Samsung Galaxy) frequently asks for insurance against theft or for insurance covering screen or battery replacement. Similarly, customers purchasing new-generation laptops or digital cameras often purchase integrative training courses (sometimes online video) to get the most from their new product.

Finally, an additional way to generate new value may be represented by offering customers the possibility to customize their products online. Modern customers are, in fact, highly interested in product customization. Accordingly, customers may customize a product online before the final shipping (www.optinmoster.com). Customers will pay for the customization service; thus, they will generate extra value for the company. Taking back the example of metaverse platforms, several brands exploit online virtual showrooms to advertise their digital products, which customers might entirely co-create. For instance, MetaVRse[2] is a 3D creation platform allowing companies to showcase their products in a virtual showroom (called 'TheMall') where brands such as Apple and Nike have already introduced their products. One of the most interesting features of these digital platforms is that users might co-create and codesign the product of their favorite brand by adding extra features, changing colors, modifying shapes, inserting logos, and so on. It clearly emerges that such a level of ad hoc customization was impossible. Moreover, the level of active engagement experienced by the consumer personalizing the product in its minimal features is critical to increasing conversions and creating advocacy.

Integrate Digital Technologies Into Existing Physical Stores

Integrating digital technologies into physical stores may enable SMEs to change their value proposition. Technologies such as interactive displays or augmented reality (AR) may allow SMEs to sell more products or services to customers visiting physical stores. Just imagine the potential of such technologies in terms of the purchase suggestions/options they may provide customers. Indeed, an interactive display or AR may suggest to customers where to find additional physical products, potential opportunities for their purchases (i.e., sales promotions), or another service they may purchase with the product. Salespersons may also help in this

[2] See: https://metavrse.com/.

perspective, but it has been observed how customers (young customers in particular) tend to follow the suggestions from technologies more. Similarly, the possibility of customers purchasing something with a click on a display or a device for AR is more appealing than compiling any paperwork (i.e., buying insurance on a product). As any purchase from customers may generate value, adding any technology capable of increasing the sales of products or services may influence SMEs' value proposition (Pizzi et al., 2019).

Changing the value proposition more than implementing new technologies (such as starting to offer digital products) is needed to thrive in the competitive digital arena. Indeed, the whole business model needs to be changed in most cases to make technologies create the maximum possible value. Accordingly, most traditional SMEs will have to change their business model by changing their competitive positioning.

Reimagine Brick-and-Mortar Positioning

Traditional brick-and-mortar SMEs were the typology of businesses most affected by the emergence of digital technologies. On the one hand, new customers' preference for online shopping significantly affected smaller players (i.e., shops on the main streets). Smaller brick-and-mortar players may not have huge assortments of products either due to space or economic constraints (Faraoni, Rialti, Zollo, & Pellicelli, 2018). A smaller traditional company is not able to store vast stocks of different products and is also not capable of affording them. On the other hand, large-scale companies were also significantly affected by the emergence of digital technologies. However, concerning what happens to smaller companies, digital technologies have a double effect on large-scale ones. The first effect of digital technologies on large-scale companies was the progressive reduction in the sales volume of their traditional physical stores. Customers started to purchase an increasing number of products daily on digital channels. The second effect was a rush toward adopting new in-store digital technologies to increase customer satisfaction and, consequently, sales.

It rapidly emerged how traditional SMEs faced the choice between adapting to digital technologies or going under. The extreme rigidity of SMEs' business models to change often caused their bankruptcy. Old ways of running a business, like old habits, die hard. Hence, it emerged because many SMEs couldn't succeed in the dawn of digital technology emergence. Such a phenomenon has been called the 'retail apocalypse'. In detail, marketing scholars have used such expressions to describe the frequent closure of many physical stores between 2010 and 2018. This apocalypse started in the USA immediately after that financial crisis. However, over more recent times, it has also begun to affect Europe. UK SMEs were the first affected, and the phenomenon diffused in continental Europe. Blockbuster and Toys 'R' Us were the most famous victims of such an apocalypse. Both company chains were obliged to declare bankruptcy, close most of their physical stores, and liquidate their assets. The emergence of digital players capable of eroding the market shares of traditional SMEs, even if tied up to the shrinkage of the middle class related to the financial crisis, was the principal cause of most of the demises in this industry. Accordingly, the retail apocalypse was one of the few cases of industry demise not related directly to poor management.

While the retail apocalypse is still occurring, it is still possible to identify many cases in which traditional SMEs survived, even amid the emergence of digital technologies. Therefore, how did some SMEs survive during the crisis storm? There is only one correct answer to this question; they changed their positioning by transforming themselves.

Suitably, it is possible to observe how some traditional SMEs started to adopt hybrid business models. Indeed, on the one hand, they continued to operate as traditional SMEs with physical stores. On the other hand, they exploited existing platforms or developed new in-house platforms to trade goods on the Internet. Therefore, some traditional SMEs developed ad hoc business units behaving as e-tailer channels to meet consumers' preferences for e-commerce platforms. In any case, to better understand how they survived and how this changed the shape of the retail industry, it is necessary to identify what e-commerce is.

Recently, e-commerce has been acknowledged by the literature as a new business model for SMEs that includes communication, information, transaction, and data exchange and reduces the limits of time and space. Similarly, e-commerce has been defined as the ensemble of activities to buy or sell a product or to exchange valuable data using an internet-based platform or a point of touch (Kim & Niehm, 2009). Electronic marketplaces, specialized e-commerce websites, smartphone applications, and online auctions are the most common examples of the abovementioned platforms or touch points. Generically speaking, thus going further than the retail horizon, according to the literature, six forms of e-commerce exist. B2C e-commerce is the form that involves the selling of a product from an e-tailer to a plethora of potential online customers (Kim & Niehm, 2009). B2B is an e-commerce form based on product exchange (i.e., spare parts) between businesses using an online platform (Gordini & Veglio, 2017). C2C is the form based on the exchange of products between individual customers (Wu et al., 2015). Next, C2B is e-commerce, where consumers make their products available online for companies to bid on and purchase (Wang et al., 2016). Finally, other forms of e-commerce involving public administrations are progressively emerging, such as C2A and B2A (Faraoni, Rialti, Zollo, & Pellicelli, 2018).

Regarding the evolution of the marketing industry, B2C is the most interesting e-commerce form for any SME wishing to be competitive in the digital arena. It is also the most basic form of e-commerce in terms of total online transactions (Turban et al., 2017). Books, digital music files, and high-tech products have long represented the most available products worldwide on online platforms (Rafiq et al., 2013). However, over the last decade, any product has become available on e-commerce platforms. Coherently, the popularity of B2C e-commerce has grown steadily among all customer cohorts (even if millennials hold the lion's share of e-commerce use). First, it has become popular due to the availability of high-speed internet connections, smartphones and tablets, and ever-more user-friendly e-commerce platforms (Yadav & Pavlou, 2014). Next, it became popular, as customers could purchase a greater choice of any product at usually lower prices (Rafiq et al., 2013).

Moving from this, it emerged that using e-commerce platforms is the greatest challenge ever for traditional SMEs. However, to maintain a competitive edge over emerging digital rivals, brick-and-mortar companies must pay attention to e-commerce implementation (Scuotto et al., 2017). To meet new customer preferences and compete with a fully-fledged e-tailer, traditional SMEs are obliged to evolve their business models in a hybrid manner by developing business units acting as e-tailers dedicated exclusively to e-commerce.

E-commerce can be beneficial for traditional, mostly brick and mortars to survive. Such platforms, first, will allow SMEs to reach new customers living where physical stores are absent. Similarly, such media will force SMEs to have different customer prices. Third, they will also allow companies to develop promotions to sell stocks of unsold products.

While large-scale players were usually the most prone to adopt e-commerce, small players may also benefit from it. Counterintuitively, e-commerce may affect small players at most. Specifically, small players capable of developing e-commerce platforms may expand dramatically, as they may start to distribute their products to customers unaware of the existence of such stores. Finally, adopting e-commerce may allow SMEs to accept common payment options existing today, such as PayPal. The adoption of e-commerce may make customers more prone to purchase something, as many new digital payment forms are more secure or flexible than traditional ones.

The two best ways to implement e-commerce exist. The first is the development mentioned above of internal e-commerce platforms. The second is to start selling their products with the help of agreements with existing players. Amazon, eBay, and similar platforms allow small companies to sell their products through existing and well-known platforms. Indeed, the first solution allows SMEs to control more of the online channel. However, the second is a cheaper and less risky way to exploit an online channel.

Regardless, it is relevant to note that using e-commerce platforms does not allow us to monitor consumers during their purchases as in the real world. Therefore, to improve online consumer engagement, it is necessary to implement systems enabling control of the online path consumers take to understand their feelings in response to online stimuli. Indeed, in the online context, sales agents influencing consumers are not present, and it is necessary to understand what makes consumers feel comfortable online and what is disappointing to them. Apart from the analytics above systems, a way to foster customers' purchases online may be developing platforms capable of allowing purchase processes to be more coherent with the new way customers are developing their purchase decisions. Thus, marketers should be more aware of the latest customer digital journey.

Finally, the transition from a traditional offline/physical brick-and-mortar approach toward what the digital scenario increasingly requires, such as a 'click-and-mortar' approach, is an element worth investigating for SMEs' survival. As previously stated in this chapter, SMEs cannot survive in the long run without at least some type of online presence in digital environments. The transition ranges from full brick-and-mortar models to full online models, passing through click-and-mortar models, which assumes critical relevance, especially in our post-pandemic era. The primary rationale underlying this transition is the way an SME's products or services are sold to the customer, either in traditional channels such as physical shops or digital channels such as online e-commerce websites. In the following, we will highlight the main advantages of opting for a hybrid strategy, which refers to the click-and-mortar approach. First, it is important to stress that customers increasingly require omnichannel strategy. Omnichannel means providing a seamless brand experience across several marketing channels, spanning from social media presence to more traditional channels. The most crucial element is ensuring the same brand experience regardless of the marketing channel used by the SME. Hence, when a consumer tries a product in a physical shop, it is very likely that the final decision to purchase will happen in a different location, such as in the online realm. This is why SMEs must anticipate this new 'phygital' journey and offer the consumer the possibility of postponing the purchase at a later moment and different location, for example, providing the opportunity to better customize online the product tried offline. Regardless of the site (offline or online), the same brand experience must be provided, which is why the interaction design of multiple touchpoints across the customer journey becomes very relevant.

Conversely, suppose a consumer lands on a website of a company being interested in a product that must be experienced offline before the final purchase. In that case, the SME will have to already design a perfectly matching journey made of both an online presence and, later, a physical touchpoint with the prospect, such as an offline showroom or shop where the consideration stage might be turned into the conversion/

purchase stage. If an SME can implement this omnichannel presence on its own, this is the best scenario for improving the customer experience across the different physical and online touchpoints of the journey. If this is too expensive, partnering with companies that are responsible for creating and managing offline or online interactions with customers is essential.

References

Aaker, D. (2015). Four ways digital works to build brands and relationships. *Journal of Brand Strategy, 4*(1), 37–48.

Akter, S., Wamba, S. F., Gunasekaran, A., Dubey, R., & Childe, S. J. (2016). How to improve firm performance using big data analytics capability and business strategy alignment? *International Journal of Production Economics, 182*, 113–131.

Apaolaza, V., He, J., & Hartmann, P. (2014). The effect of gratifications derived from use of the social networking site Qzone on Chinese adolescents' positive mood. *Computers in Human Behavior, 41*, 203–211.

Bergman, S. M., Fearrington, M. E., Davenport, S. W., & Bergman, J. Z. (2011). Millennials, narcissism, and social networking: What narcissists do on social networking sites and why. *Personality and Individual Differences, 50*(5), 706–711.

Brakus, J. J., Schmitt, B. H., & Zarantonello, L. (2009). Brand experience: What is it? How is it measured? Does it affect loyalty? *Journal of Marketing, 73*(3), 52–68.

Camilleri, M. A. (2018). Market segmentation, targeting and positioning. In *Travel marketing, tourism economics and the airline product* (pp. 69–83). Springer.

Chaffey, D., & Ellis-Chadwick, F. (2016). *Digital marketing: Strategy, implementation and practice*. Pearson Education.

Chen, C., Ma, J., Susilo, Y., Liu, Y., & Wang, M. (2016). The promises of big data and small data for travel behavior (aka human mobility) analysis. *Transportation Research Part C: Emerging Technologies, 68*, 285–299.

Chen, H., Chiang, R. H., & Storey, V. C. (2012). Business intelligence and analytics: From big data to big impact. *MIS Quarterly, 36*(4), 1165–1188.

Chohan, R., & Paschen, J. (2021). What marketers need to know about non-fungible tokens (NFTs). *Business Horizons*. https://doi.org/10.1016/j.bushor.2021.12.004

Cialdini, R. B. (1993). *Influence: The psychology of persuasion*. Morrow.
Couldry, N., & Turow, J. (2014). Advertising, big data and the clearance of the public realm: Marketers' new approaches to the content subsidy. *International Journal of Communication, 8*, 1710–1726.
Crane, A. (2005). In the company of spies: When competitive intelligence gathering becomes industrial espionage. *Business Horizons, 48*(3), 233–240.
Davenport, T. H., Barth, P., & Bean, R. (2012). How 'big data' is different. *MIT Sloan Management Review*.
Di Benedetto, C. A., & Kim, K. H. (2016). Customer equity and value management of global brands: Bridging theory and practice from financial and marketing perspectives: Introduction to a Journal of Business Research Special Section. *Journal of Business Research, 69*, 3721–3724.
Dishman, P. L., & Calof, J. L. (2008). Competitive intelligence: A multiphasic precedent to marketing strategy. *European Journal of Marketing, 42*(7/8), 766–785.
Edelman, D. C. (2010). Branding in the digital age. *Harvard Business Review, 88*(12), 62–69.
Erevelles, S., Fukawa, N., & Swayne, L. (2016). Big Data consumer analytics and the transformation of marketing. *Journal of Business Research, 69*(2), 897–904.
Faraoni, M., Rialti, R., Zollo, L., & Pellicelli, A. C. (2018). Exploring e-loyalty antecedents in B2C e-commerce: Empirical results from Italian grocery retailers. *British Food Journal*. https://doi.org/10.1108/BFJ-04-2018-0216
Flavián, C., & Guinalíu, M. (2006). Consumer trust, perceived security and privacy policy: Three basic elements of loyalty to a web site. *Industrial Management & Data Systems, 106*(5), 601–620.
Fournier, S., & Avery, J. (2011). The uninvited brand. *Business Horizons, 54*(3), 193–207.
Fromm, J., & Garton, C. (2013). *Marketing to millennials: Reach the largest and most influential generation of consumers ever*. AMACOM Division of American Management Association.
Fu, J. R., Lu, I. W., Chen, J. H., & Farn, C. K. (2020). Investigating consumers' online social shopping intention: An information processing perspective. *International Journal of Information Management, 54*, 102189.
Gandomi, A., & Haider, M. (2015). Beyond the hype: Big data concepts, methods, and analytics. *International Journal of Information Management, 35*(2), 137–144.
Gao, Q., & Feng, C. (2016). Branding with social media: User gratifications, usage patterns, and brand message content strategies. *Computers in Human Behavior, 63*, 868–890.

Gensler, S., Völckner, F., Liu-Thompkins, Y., & Wiertz, C. (2013). Managing brands in the social media environment. *Journal of Interactive Marketing, 27*(4), 242–256.
Gordini, N., & Veglio, V. (2017). Customers churn prediction and marketing retention strategies. An application of support vector machines based on the AUC parameter-selection technique in B2B e-commerce industry. *Industrial Marketing Management, 62*, 100–107.
Gupta, A., Deokar, A., Iyer, L., Sharda, R., & Schrader, D. (2018). Big data & analytics for societal impact: Recent research and trends. *Information Systems Frontiers, 20*(2), 185–194.
Hamzah, Z. L., Alwi, S. F. S., & Othman, M. N. (2014). Designing corporate brand experience in an online context: A qualitative insight. *Journal of Business Research, 67*, 2299–2310.
Hatch, M. J., & Schultz, M. (2010). Toward a theory of brand co-creation with implications for brand governance. *Journal of Brand Management, 17*(8), 590–604.
Hofstetter, R., de Bellis, E., Brandes, L., Clegg, M., Lamberton, C., Reibstein, D., et al. (2022). Crypto-marketing: How non-fungible tokens (NFTs) challenge traditional marketing. *Marketing Letters, 33*(4), 705–711.
Johnson, M. W., Christensen, C. M., & Kagermann, H. (2008). Reinventing your business model. *Harvard Business Review, 86*(12), 57–68.
Jourdan, Z., Rainer, R. K., & Marshall, T. E. (2008). Business intelligence: An analysis of the literature. *Information Systems Management, 25*(2), 121–131.
Kaplan, A. M., & Haenlein, M. (2010). Users of the world, unite! The challenges and opportunities of social media. *Business Horizons, 53*(1), 59–68.
Karafiloski, E., & Mishev, A. (2017, July). Blockchain solutions for big data challenges: A literature review. In *IEEE EUROCON 2017-17th international conference on Smart Technologies* (pp. 763–768). IEEE.
Karapanos, E., Teixeira, P., & Gouveia, R. (2016). Need fulfillment and experiences on social media: A case on Facebook and WhatsApp. *Computers in Human Behavior, 55*, 888–897.
Kim, A. J., & Ko, E. (2012). Do social media marketing activities enhance customer equity? An empirical study of luxury fashion brand. *Journal of Business Research, 65*(10), 1480–1486.
Kim, H., & Niehm, L. S. (2009). The impact of website quality on information quality, value, and loyalty intentions in apparel retailing. *Journal of Interactive Marketing, 23*(3), 221–233.
Kim, K. H., & Moon, H. (2021). Innovative digital marketing management in B2B markets. *Industrial Marketing Management, 95*, 1–4.

Kim, S., & Stoel, L. (2004). Dimensional hierarchy of retail website quality. *Information & Management, 41*(5), 619–633.
Kimble, C., & Milolidakis, G. (2015). Big data and business intelligence: Debunking the myths. *Global Business and Organizational Excellence, 35*(1), 23–34.
Ko, E., Kim, E. Y., Taylor, C. R., Kim, K. H., & Kang, I. J. (2007). Cross-national market segmentation in the fashion industry: A study of European, Korean, and US consumers. *International Marketing Review, 24*, 629–651.
Kumar, A., & Lim, H. (2008). Age differences in mobile service perceptions: Comparison of generation Y and baby boomers. *Journal of Services Marketing, 22*(7), 568–577.
Labrinidis, A., & Jagadish, H. V. (2012). Challenges and opportunities with big data. *Proceedings of the VLDB Endowment, 5*(12), 2032–2033.
Lemon, K. N., & Verhoef, P. C. (2016). Understanding customer experience throughout the customer journey. *Journal of Marketing, 80*(6), 69–96.
Lien, C. H., & Cao, Y. (2014). Examining WeChat users' motivations, trust, attitudes, and positive word-of-mouth: Evidence from China. *Computers in Human Behavior, 41*, 104–111.
Marcussen, C. H. (1999). The effects of internet distribution of travel and tourism services on the marketing mix: No-frills, fair fares, and fare wars in the air. *Information Technology & Tourism, 2*(3), 197–212.
McAfee, A., & Brynjolfsson, E. (2012). Big data: The management revolution. *Harvard Business Review, 90*(10), 60–68.
McAlexander, J. H., Schouten, J. W., & Koenig, H. F. (2002). Building brand community. *Journal of Marketing, 66*(1), 38–54.
Mishra, D., Luo, Z., Jiang, S., Papadopoulos, T., & Dubey, R. (2017). A bibliographic study on big data: Concepts, trends and challenges. *Business Process Management Journal, 23*(3), 555–573.
Nosi, C., Zollo, L., Rialti, R., & Ciappei, C. (2022). Why do consumers free ride? Investigating the effects of cognitive effort on postpurchase dissonance. *Journal of Consumer Marketing, 39*(5), 417–431.
Pizzi, G., Scarpi, D., Pichierri, M., & Vannucci, V. (2019). Virtual reality, real reactions?: Comparing consumers' perceptions and shopping orientation across physical and virtual-reality retail stores. *Computers in Human Behavior, 96*, 1–12.
Prilop, M., Tonisson, L., & Maicher, L. (2013). Designing analytical approaches for interactive competitive intelligence. *International Journal of Service Science, Management, Engineering, and Technology (IJSSMET), 4*(2), 34–45.

Rafiq, M., Fulford, H., & Lu, X. (2013). Building customer loyalty in online retailing: The role of relationship quality. *Journal of Marketing Management, 29*(3–4), 494–517.

Ramaswamy, V., & Ozcan, K. (2016). Brand value co-creation in a digitalized world: An integrative framework and research implications. *International Journal of Research in Marketing, 33*(1), 93–106.

Rialti, R., Caliandro, A., Zollo, L., & Ciappei, C. (2018). Co-creation experiences in social media brand communities: Analyzing the main types of co-created experiences. *Spanish Journal of Marketing-ESIC, 22*(2), 122–141.

Rialti, R., Filieri, R., Zollo, L., Bazi, S., & Ciappei, C. (2022). Assessing the relationship between gamified advertising and in-app purchases: A consumers' benefits-based perspective. *International Journal of Advertising, 41*, 1–23. https://doi.org/10.1080/02650487.2022.2025735

Rialti, R., Marzi, G., Ciappei, C., & Busso, D. (2019). Big data and dynamic capabilities: A bibliometric analysis and systematic literature review. *Management Decision*. https://doi.org/10.1108/MD-07-2018-0821

Rialti, R., Marzi, G., Ciappei, C., & Caputo, A. (2018). Reframing agile organization. Does big data analytics capabilities matter?. *Academy of Management Global Proceedings, Surrey*, 1–8.

Rialti, R., Zollo, L., Caliandro, A., & Ciappei, C. (2016). Social media strategies to protect brand image and corporate reputation in the digital era: A digital investigation of the Eni vs. Report case. *Mercati & Competitività, 4*, 65–84.

Rialti, R., Zollo, L., Pellegrini, M. M., & Ciappei, C. (2017). Exploring the antecedents of brand loyalty and electronic word of mouth in social-media-based brand communities: Do gender differences matter? *Journal of Global Marketing, 30*(3), 147–160.

Roberts, J. A., & Manolis, C. (2000). Baby boomers and busters: An exploratory investigation of attitudes toward marketing, advertising and consumerism. *Journal of Consumer Marketing, 17*(6), 481–497.

Santoro, G., Fiano, F., Bertoldi, B., & Ciampi, F. (2018). Big data for business management in the retail industry. *Management Decision*. https://doi.org/10.1108/MD-07-2018-0829

Scuotto, V., Caputo, F., Villasalero, M., & Del Giudice, M. (2017). A multiple buyer–supplier relationship in the context of SMEs' digital supply chain management. *Production Planning & Control, 28*(16), 1378–1388.

Søilen, K. S. (2017). Why care about competitive intelligence and market intelligence? The case of Ericsson and the Swedish Cellulose Company. *Journal of Intelligence Studies in Business, 7*(2), 27–39.

Statista. (2021). Population distribution in the United States in 2021, by generation. Retrieved December 20, 2022, from https://www.statista.com/statistics/296974/us-population-share-by-generation/

Stewart, J. S., Oliver, E. G., Cravens, K. S., & Oishi, S. (2017). Managing millennials: Embracing generational differences. *Business Horizons, 60*, 45–54.

Taken Smith, K. (2012). Longitudinal study of digital marketing strategies targeting Millennials. *Journal of Consumer Marketing, 29*(2), 86–92.

Taken Smith, K., & Brower, T. R. (2012). Longitudinal study of green marketing strategies that influence Millennials. *Journal of Strategic Marketing, 20*(6), 535–551.

Tallon, P. P., & Pinsonneault, A. (2011). Competing perspectives on the link between strategic information technology alignment and organizational agility: Insights from a mediation model. *MIS Quarterly, 35*(2), 463–486.

Thampanya, N., Nasir, M. A., & Huynh, T. L. D. (2020). Asymmetric correlation and hedging effectiveness of gold & cryptocurrencies: From preindustrial to the 4th industrial revolution. *Technological Forecasting and Social Change, 159*, 120195.

Troise, C., Corvello, V., Ghobadian, A., & O'Regan, N. (2022). How can SMEs successfully navigate VUCA environment: The role of agility in the digital transformation era. *Technological Forecasting and Social Change, 174*, 121227.

Tsai, S. P. (2014). Love and satisfaction drive persistent stickiness: Investigating international tourist hotel brands. *International Journal of Tourism Research, 16*(6), 565–577.

Turban, E., Outland, J., King, D., Lee, J. K., Liang, T. P., & Turban, D. C. (2017). *Electronic commerce 2018: A managerial and social networks perspective*. Springer.

Turner, A. (2015). Generation Z: Technology and social interest. *The Journal of Individual Psychology, 71*(2), 103–113.

Verhagen, T., Swen, E., Feldberg, F., & Merikivi, J. (2015). Benefitting from virtual customer environments: An empirical study of customer engagement. *Computers in Human Behavior, 48*, 340–357.

Wamba, S. F., Akter, S., Edwards, A., Chopin, G., & Gnanzou, D. (2015). How 'big data' can make big impact: Findings from a systematic review and a longitudinal case study. *International Journal of Production Economics, 165*, 234–246.

Wamba, S. F., & Mishra, D. (2017). Big data integration with business processes: A literature review. *Business Process Management Journal, 23*(3), 477–492.

Wang, W. T., Wang, Y. S., & Liu, E. R. (2016). The stickiness intention of group-buying websites: The integration of the commitment–trust theory and e-commerce success model. *Information & Management, 53*(5), 625–642.

Wayne, M. L. (2018). Netflix, Amazon, and branded television content in subscription video on-demand portals. *Media, Culture & Society, 40*(5), 725–741.

Wright, S., & Calof, J. L. (2006). The quest for competitive, business and marketing intelligence: A country comparison of current practices. *European Journal of Marketing, 40*(5/6), 453–465.

Wu, K., Vassileva, J., Noorian, Z., & Zhao, Y. (2015). How do you feel when you see a list of prices? The interplay among price dispersion, perceived risk and initial trust in Chinese C2C market. *Journal of Retailing and Consumer Services, 25*, 36–46.

Yadav, M. S., & Pavlou, P. A. (2014). Marketing in computer-mediated environments: Research synthesis and new directions. *Journal of Marketing, 78*(1), 20–40.

Yin, S., & Kaynak, O. (2015). Big data for modern industry: Challenges and trends [point of view]. *Proceedings of the IEEE, 103*(2), 143–146.

Yoon, S. (2013). Do negative consumption experiences hurt manufacturers or retailer? *Psychology & Marketing, 30*, 555–565.

Zarantonello, L., & Schmitt, B. H. (2010). Using the brand experience scale to profile consumers and predict consumer behaviour. *Journal of Brand Management, 17*, 532–540.

Zollo, L., Carranza, R., Faraoni, M., Díaz, E., & Martín-Consuegra, D. (2021). What influences consumers' intention to purchase organic personal care products? The role of social reassurance. *Journal of Retailing and Consumer Services, 60*, 102432.

Zollo, L., Filieri, R., Rialti, R., & Yoon, S. (2020). Unpacking the relationship between social media marketing and brand equity: The mediating role of consumers' benefits and experience. *Journal of Business Research, 117*, 256–267.

Zollo, L., Rialti, R., Marrucci, A., & Ciappei, C. (2022). How do museums foster loyalty in tech-savvy visitors? The role of social media and digital experience. *Current Issues in Tourism, 25*(18), 2991–3008.

5

Case Studies: From Theory to Practice

The book's previous chapters observed the principal macro-factors influencing the intention of SMEs to digitalize the top technologies that make digital transformation possible, and how modern consumer behaviors are pushing SMEs to digitalize. It is also relevant to evaluate how these factors wrap up with the endogenous traits of businesses and how managers could approach a digital transformation of marketing strategies purposefully and effectively. It is relevant to understand which strategies companies use to readjust their organizational structures to integrate new technologies into their marketing strategies and what effects these strategies generate on internal procedures. Likewise, a greater focus on the main strategic outcomes of this kind of transformation according to diverse businesses is needed.

Therefore, this book will try to provide answers to the following questions:

Q1: *Which are the primary triggers underlying digital transformation in SMEs?*

Q2: *How do SMEs reshape their process to embrace Industry 4.0 technologies in marketing strategies?*

Q3: *What are the principal outcomes of the transformation process?*

R. Rialti, L. Zollo, *Digital Transformation of SME Marketing Strategies*,
https://doi.org/10.1007/978-3-031-33646-1_5

To attempt to answer these questions, C-suite members and managers of five SMEs operating in diverse industries were interviewed. In detail, a case study approach rooted in semi-structured interviews concerning several specific areas of SMEs' marketing strategies has been selected.

5.1 Methodological Approach

The book's objective is to shed some light on the dynamics underlying SMEs' willingness to embrace the digital transformation of marketing strategies. In particular, the expected outcome pertains to developing a framework capable of providing managers with a graphical map capable of helping them select and implement the right technology for their case. In such regard, the theoretical observation must be reinforced by findings from real-world cases of SMEs that successfully transformed digitally (Scuotto et al., 2021). Such an approach may allow greater penetration into the phenomenon, a practice-oriented view, the development of new strategies, and the possibility to obtain a greater generalization.

The primary theoretical lens that we will use to build the following empirical chapter is the institutional theory (DiMaggio & Powell, 1991; Scott, 2008). According to the organizational perspective, institutional theory aims to understand how organizations' social structures, norms, and behaviors change, transform, and evolve in pursuit of legitimacy and efficiency based on their institutional environment and ecosystem (Yang & Su, 2014). Thus, companies reorganize their market approach to maximize their goals while gaining institutional approval—from a macro-, meso-, and micro-perspective—which allows them to become increasingly competitive sustainably. As a result, institutional embeddedness requires adaptation toward a dynamic market characterized by unpredictable social actors' moves and social structure constraints. Therefore, firms may adopt multiple identities or configurations, always looking for a balance and alignment between organizational identity (i.e., the way the company wants to be perceived in the institutional environment through its culture, values, mission, and vision) and organizational image (i.e., the way institutions perceive the company). In a marketing fashion, this identity-image fit is well expressed by the notion of brand identity and brand image alignment (Ranfagni et al., 2021). The main risk resulting from a brand identity-image misalignment is a loss of brand reputation, customer dissatisfaction, and a decrease in brand equity. Therefore, building a positive institutional network is becoming increasingly important for marketers. We summarize the crucial role of institutional theory in marketing in Fig. 5.1, which allows marketers to answer a crucial question: *What are the successful strategic responses the company should implement to sustain its competitive advantage in the institutional environment?*

As shown in Fig. 5.1, successfully managing the trade-offs and conflicting interests among all the social actors, institutional rules, and market dynamics is the main challenge for marketers attempting to transform their companies digitally and innovatively. Adaptation to a new business model logic and, at the same time, consistency with the company's original identity are key enablers of success in the modern unpredictable, and fast-changing institutional environment that we are facing. Macro-drivers

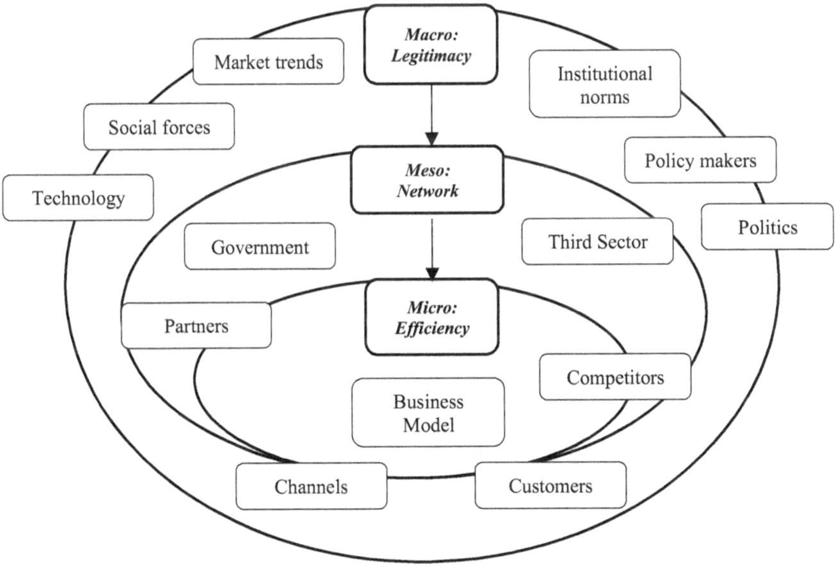

Fig. 5.1 Institutional ecosystem from a marketing perspective. Source: Authors' Elaboration

and social forces refer to the ecosystem's technological, social, and political norms imposing the company's adaptation to such an environment to reach institutional legitimization. Meso-social actors are governmental institutions, society (Third Sector), and business partners representing potential strategic alliances that result in a strong network for future growth. This is especially true if considering collaborations with partners enabling digitalization processes for the company. Microelements are the drivers of revenue generation—such as customers and innovative channels—and the elements impacting the cost structure—such as employees and key resources. These drivers and factors should result in efficient business model functioning.

The recent paradigmatic shift imposed by technological innovations, such as I4.0, and negative environmental crises, such as the COVID-19 pandemic, requires marketers to face new institutional opportunities and challenges. We will focus on how the digital transformation and transition of SMEs' economic and management ecosystem has set new 'rules of the game' regarding production, exchange, and distribution logics (Yang & Su, 2014). To gain legitimacy and sustain competitive advantage concerning the institutional logics affecting SMEs' ecosystems, managers and marketers need to design, implement, and govern effective strategies (Zollo, Pellegrini et al., 2022). An example of an adaptation strategy that SMEs opted for, especially during and after the 2020 pandemic outburst, refers to a new way to manage relationships with customers, which represent one of the most important 'external' institutional agents (macro- and meso-social actors in Fig. 5.1) of change for companies, along with 'internal stakeholders' (micro-social actors) such as employees (Gervasi, Faldetta, & Zollo, 2022; Gervasi, Faldetta, Zollo, & Lombardi, 2022). This is the main rationale that led to the rising phenomenon of 'digital twins' in marketing (Wang et al., 2021).

A digital twin is a virtual representation of a customer's digital avatar. SMEs might exploit these online, virtual, digital representations to test their new products or services against their targeted buyer persona (Vijayakumar, 2020). The main goal is to simulate and forecast customers' reactions, outcomes, and feedback after using the company's new product. Digital customer experience is one of the most promising areas in marketing and consumer behavior research, mainly because modern customers have increasingly higher expectations concerning brand experience, so it becomes vital for SMEs to adapt to such institutional requirements and gain legitimacy from their environmental socioeconomic agents (Rialti et al., 2020). Moreover, SMEs might anticipate customers' latent needs, thanks to these virtual A/B testing opportunities, which require an advanced data gathering and management capability.

As we have stressed in Fig. 5.1, the modern digital customer journey requires SMEs to be highly competitive in their institutional environment, designing and managing effective interactions, relationships, and touchpoints with many social agents impacting their business model (i.e., suppliers, competitors, clients, public entities, etc.). To optimize the customer journey—meaning obtaining more conversions from leads to prospects to customers across the different stages—digital simulations of buyer personas' behavior are a strategic option for SME marketers. Naturally, digital versions of any other stakeholders in the institutional environment might prove beneficial, and this is how marketers should exploit new technologies and digital tools of I4.0.

To perform an in-depth investigation of singular organizational responses to numerous identities in terms of corporate design, the multiple case study method has been deemed the most appropriate. Indeed, as the problems investigated by the research are qualitative in nature and the literature is quite limited, this methodology is recommended by existing works. We analyzed three cases in our study to externally validate and strengthen the results from a single case study (within-case analysis) with a cross-case comparison (between-case analysis). Theoretical saturation was reached as the findings started to converge toward the same results. Our qualitative analysis was integrated with theoretical opinions related to the observed phenomena, and we consciously bid to set relevant examples although our data.

The field data provided real-world proofs, and elements of the evolving framework were revised and enhanced periodically as the analysis moved iteratively between empirical findings and conceptual developments, thanks to the so-called reflective spiral. This interaction of emergent theory and data collection generated our final framework for explaining strategies pursued by SMEs that decide to digitalize their business, which is presented in the next chapter.

From a practical point of view, we draw our insights through a sample of businesses identified through their emerging marketing campaigns. We focused on businesses whose innovative marketing strategies were praised as particularly creative by critics and competitors operating within the same industry (Krings et al., 2021). Cases of businesses operating in B2C and B2B contexts were selected together, as 4.0-oriented digital transformation is a cross-industry and cross-strategy phenomenon and considering two typologies of companies proved useful to understand the internal micro-mechanisms more in depth (Ardito et al., 2018). At this point, to collect our data and develop a text corpus, we first checked the availability of secondary data, such as organizations' publications, social reports, codes of ethics, publicly available statutes, and websites, to allow for triangulation of data. Second, we considered the accessibility to primary data ensured by the lively engagement of presidents and managers; this allowed researchers to have multiple rounds of feedback. Next, we concretely verified through real-world observation that organizations implemented 4.0-oriented marketing strategies and that such communication was not only a façade. Specifically, in our study, as a proxy of this strategic behavior, we observed a factor indicating the actual implementation of these strategies, namely, the implementation of at least two technologies within strategies addressing customers. Likewise, we checked whether the implemented technologies had a real impact on business marketing strategies. Therefore, we checked that such generating activities were not simply limited to some sporadic events but integrated within business strategies. Evidence about the selected businesses is shown in Table 5.1.

Consistent with inductive research principles, to ensure the achievement of the explained theoretical saturation of the emerging findings from the sample, we selected a diversified sample of SMEs that integrated 4.0 technologies into their marketing strategies. Aside from allowing a greater generalization, the selection of SMEs operating in diverse industries allowed us to understand common patterns characterizing digital transformation in SMEs in more detail. Five SMEs from industrialized regions of Italy were selected to observe the phenomenon in detail. In such a regard, SMEs in Italy represent a relevant context for investigation. First, SMEs in Italy represent the most significant chunk of businesses in

Table 5.1 Selected SMEs

Name	HQs	Employees	Year of foundation	Industry	Principal sources	
					Primary	Secondary
Alpha	Arezzo (AR), Tuscany, Italy	200	1978	Fashion components and garments (mostly B2B)	Three interviews (CEO, general director, marketing director) Direct observation	1. Internal magazine 2. Stakeholder reports 3. Shareholders report 4. Corporate website 5. Institutional communication 6. Academic papers on the same case
Beta	Milan, Lombardy, Italy	50	2015	Food and wine	Five interviews (CEO, CFO, marketing eirector) Direct observation	1. Shareholder reports 2. Stakeholder reports 3. Corporate website 4. Institutional communication 5. Academic papers on the same case
Gamma	Milan, Lombardy, Italy	100	2013	FinTech	Three interviews (Founders, CEO, marketing director) Direct observation	1. Internal magazine 2. Stakeholder reports 3. Shareholders report 4. Corporate website 5. Institutional communication 6. Practitioners' report on similar business cases

(*continued*)

Table 5.1 (continued)

Name	HQs	Employees	Year of foundation	Industry	Principal sources	
					Primary	Secondary
Delta	Florence, Tuscany, Italy	50	1987	Fashion distribution	Two Interviews (CEO, junior marketing director)	1. Shareholder reports 2. Stakeholder reports 3. Corporate website 4. Physical stores layout and digital stores architecture
Theta	Verona, Veneto, Italy	60	1970	Home décor and furniture	Three interview (CEO, marketing manager, product manager)	1. Stakeholder reports 2. Shareholders report 3. Corporate website 4. Institutional communication

Source: Authors' elaboration

the economic panorama. Second, SMEs were frequently in a hurry than larger businesses regarding digital transformation. Large businesses were already adopting advanced methods to reach their consumers, whereas SMEs were frequently lagging and thus were wishing to close this gap. Third, many incentives existed in Italy concerning digitalization processes, and most were targeting SMEs. This theoretical sampling approach allowed us to create an experimental empirical basis to study the phenomenon under particularly insightful and revealing contexts.

5.2 Selected Cases and Data Collection

Data collection was implemented by personal interviews with SME key informants who play a strategic key role within the organization—such as CEOs, presidents, board members, and managers. Each interview lasted for at least one hour. The interviews were collected over one year (January 2022–December 2022) and were conducted by two authors of this research, and one researcher attended all of them to maintain internal consistency of the protocol. Data were updated monthly through discussions with the managers to maintain consistency over time. All the interviews were recorded and transcribed.

The interview protocol used during the data collection was kind of 'fluid' to take advantage of possible incipient themes. Such an approach is indeed consistent with the practice of semi-structured interviews. However, such a procedure was also deemed highly suitable to address a strategic topic that has somehow been addressed differently between all businesses. This notwithstanding, the following common questions were always addressed (Table 5.2).

An overall research diary was kept tracking the insights emerging during the data collection systematically. We started by inspecting all data about one single case, dumping anything that was irrelevant, and keeping what seemed more relevant. The research diaries were updated to clarify up-and-coming topics until only a few new ones occurred. As exemplar phenomena were collected, we related them to the theoretical frame to re-examine consistently.

Table 5.2 Interview protocol

Institutional Area	Environment	Evaluations concerning the environment	Selected technology	Selected implementation strategy	Strategic responses and outcomes
Interview guidelines	1. Macro-environments factors 1.a *Technological availability* 1.b *Technological environment* 1.c *Incentives to adopt technology* 2. Meso-environment 2.a *Competitive pressures* 2.b *Competitors' strategies* 3. Micro-Environment 3.a *Internal Skills* 3.b *Selected outcomes*	1. Institutional orientation 1.a *Coherence with company vision and mission* 1.b *Coherence with consumers' preferences* 2. Institutional capital 2.a *Availability of resources* 2.b *Availability of skills* 2.c *Evaluation of consistency with company culture*	1. Which one among the 4.0 basic technologies you implemented 2. Which one among the 4.0 supporting technologies you implemented	1. Which kind of implementation process was selected? 1.a Top-down 1.b Bottom-up 2. Which tools have been selected and used to monitor the transformation process? 3. Which one among strategic coupling or strategic renewal do you think is the most suitable strategy in digital transformation? 4. Which trade-offs have been made in the implementation of strategy?	1. Which outcomes does the digital transformation generate? 2. Which new competitive advantages did the company get as a consequence of the digital transformation?

Source: Author's elaboration

Interviews were then transcribed and read, with reports on emergent themes contemporaneously recorded within the research logs. Central nodes were obtained at the end of such activity, representing our main topics to develop the framework. These finely grained codes, not reported in the paper for brevity's sake, represented the base for the within-case analysis. The correlated and supporting information is drawn from secondary sources. In such a regard, the team's authors started an axial coding procedure to develop several aggregative iterations. The results of this second phase shared between the authors and the diverse patterns obtained in isolation have been compared. In this regard, the protocol described by Finch and applied to the entrepreneurial and management field by Anderson et al. was used. Henceforth, during the qualitative coding, we moved back and forth between the theory and the data; this operation was done several times as necessary to frame all the topics from the mainstream literature. This allowed an 'open mind' tactic for analyzing the data and contemporarily avoided the 'no-where heading' indication. Thus, the authors avoid the results would be completely disconnected from useful concepts and schemes derived from the literature (Rialti, Marrucci et al., 2022).

5.2.1 SMEs' Digitalization and Marketing in the Fashion Industry

Alpha is a company operating in the fashion supply chain. It produces and finishes garments and accessories for most independent fashion brands and the largest fashion group. Consistent with the vision of the CEO, the company is not outsourcing or delocalizing any production phase. The main HQ is located approximately one hour from Florence and currently employs about 300–350 people.

Because of the scaling up of the company and the mutated environment, over the last five years, the company perceived the need to restructure its marketing strategies. Advanced technology-based solutions were deemed fundamental to remain competitive.

a. **Environment**

The interviews immediately showed how the main factors triggering the need to change were represented by competitors' pressure and evolving preferences of B2B and B2C consumers. On the one hand, it was observed that competitors adopting improved communication channels and tracing instruments were the most relevant pushing factor.

Likewise, it was observed how the request from B2B consumers to better trace production phases to communicate the authenticity of the product for final consumers represents a significant push. Meso-environment characteristics thus were the ones causing the immediate perception of the need.

Macroenvironmental factors played a role. In such a regard, the CEO observed how incentives from the government to implement innovative technologies were fundamental to convincing the board of directors on the final implementation. However, some of the technologies were perceived as already available and ready. Technological availability thus was not deemed a fundamental element in the decision to adopt the technology.

b. **Evaluations of the Environment**

The main technologies implemented by *Alpha* were IoT, RFID, big data analytics (BDA), and blockchain protocols. In such a regard, these technologies were considered coherent with the vision of the company. To do so, *Alpha initially* evaluated the purposes of the project, which were first the need to communicate corporate customers' information about the production processes (which in turn were communicated to final consumers) and the need to diversify its communication strategy concerning competitors. When the purposes were coherent, the company implemented diverse technologies to help achieve the first. It was observed how the cost of investment (reduced by incentives) was coherent. Additionally, as *Alpha* has an internal IT department, it was observed that the main missing skills were related to blockchain-specific skills.

Over the last decade, *Alpha* invested significantly in developing a lean-based culture. In such a regard, managers found it extremely easy to implement a change-oriented strategy. Employee commitment emerged as fundamental to fostering the marketing 4.0 initiative.

c. **Selected Technologies**

As previously assessed, IoT, RFID, BDA, and blockchain protocols were the leading technologies implemented by *Alpha*. However, why were these specific technologies fundamental to achieving the expected results?

First, these technologies proved fundamental to tracing all the production phases regarding IoT and RFID. Likewise, they were the data generation technologies within the firm. In this regard, IoT and RFID were the technologies that allowed *Alpha* to trace all the production phases and to have fresh data to explain to corporate consumers about the production phases and ensure that all of them were done internally.

Next, BDA proved fundamental to decodifying which ones among this chuck of information were fundamental to improving how the business operated. Additionally, through BDA (and AI), it became possible for *Alpha* to understand which customers were looking at corporate pages, their motivation, and why they were looking at Alpha concerning its competitors. In this regard, the marketing managers stressed how, through BDA, he could adjust Alpha's marketing strategies to put in evidence the topics of interest for lurkers of the website (which, in this case, were Made in Italy and Sustainability).

Finally, blockchain technology was fundamental to show corporate consumers the traceability of any production phase.

d. **Selected Implementation Strategy**

The decision to implement a 4.0-oriented marketing strategy was taken from top management. However, *Alpha* undertook a process to involve most employees in such a process. The engagement proved fundamental to success.

The biggest trade-off consisted of the impossibility of realizing the entire vision of marketing managers concerning developing more advanced communication outlets (such as innovative social media) and reaping the data generated by these channels. Indeed, such a strategy could have been more suitable and fitting with corporate culture.

Strategic coupling was the selected implementation strategy. Indeed, the new tools did not revolutionize how the business operated.

Finally, in terms of tools to monitor the process, traditional project advancement KPIs were deemed sufficient to monitor the project (indeed, they did not involve final consumers directly).

e. **Strategic Responses and Outcomes**

In the end, *Alpha* increased its visibility. The effect was indirect, as it was derived from the improved information that its corporate consumers were providing to their final ones. The number of visits to the website increased dramatically as final consumers started to become curious about the supply chain processes and the possibility of understanding the origin of their purchased product through the observation of the blockchain nodes.

Notwithstanding this indirect effect, requests from corporate consumers (including new ones) increased significantly, as most deemed this kind of communication fundamentals.

Additionally, individual final consumers started to tag Alpha in their posts to show initiative and make their peers understand the importance of information in choosing a fashion product.

5.2.2 SMEs' Digitalization and Marketing in the Food and Wine Industry

Beta is an Italian SME (50 employees) operating in the food & wine sector, specifically focusing on wine delivery. Beta's entrepreneurs founded the company a few years ago in 2015. Therefore, as a young SME, the main founders aim to increase visibility not only in Lombardy, the original region but also across the country. The pandemic years—2020/2021—represented a crucial turning point for the company because while several competitors did not survive, Beta could effectively restructure and redesign their marketing channel and distribution strategies by exploiting e-commerce and online sales. The way the company rethought their channel management and marketing represents a benchmark for the industry, which is undergoing profound changes, especially after the COVID-19 consequences.

a. **Environment**

The Italian food and wine sector represents one of the quintessential natures of the country, which is famous and highly acknowledged all around the world for its unique, rare, and inimitable cuisine and chefs. Focusing on the critical issues of such an industry, the main problems refer to the mindset of entrepreneurs and founders of long-lasting companies and essential realities that, on the one hand, embody the Italian 'genius', thanks to their creativity, passion, and secret recipes, but, on the other hand, are characterized by a strong resistance to change (McDermott et al., 2013). I4.0 was rarely implemented by entrepreneurs and founders involved in the food and wine industry because they still rely on their heritage, which is their competitive advantage and obstacles to change and innovation. Therefore, *Beta* was successfully recognized as an SME able to seminally change how food and wine products and services are sold to the younger generation and the conventional customer base.

b. **Evaluations of the Environment**

The main challenge for Beta was to 'educate' Italian food and wine customers about a new way to experience the same products but in a new way, for example, through online and virtual channels. It appears to be a paradox, but the pandemic period was the perfect time to propose such a revolution: while everyone was forced to stay home during the lockdown, Italian customers still wanted to enjoy their lunch, dinners, and *aperitivo*. Hence, *Beta* implemented effective strategic communication by focusing its advertising on providing the same quality and taste as always but through delivery at home. Of course, younger customers immediately reacted positively to this new approach for an 'old' industry. Consequently, the indirect benefits that online channels and internet marketing brought to food and wine brands were clear: rebranding toward younger and broader audiences.

c. **Selected Technologies**

Effectively combining wine products and quick delivery services requires a solid digital transition of the company's marketing channels (Faraoni, Rialti, & Zollo, 2018). Therefore, the business model's building block that was primarily impacted during the digitalization process is channels and distribution. *Beta* represents a benchmark in terms of an omnichannel strategy, specifically referring to the successful way SMEs exploited integration among (1) apps, (2) websites, and (3) social media. By integrating their online presence throughout these strategic online assets carefully intertwined, *Beta*'s customers could enjoy their drinks and *aperitivo* by tasting the same old experience they were used to when buying these products in wine stores, cocktail bars, or supermarkets. In this case, technology was directed at enhancing the online experience as best as possible, aiming to shorten timing and eliminate physical barriers—thinking about the limitations of the pandemic period.

d. **Selected Implementation Strategy**

Beta's founders immediately realized the huge opportunity the food and wine market potentially offered to a new, small company with a powerful vision, such as becoming the quickest and highest-quality wine product delivery intermediary existing in the industry. As many successful stories of companies demonstrate, this is also a compelling case of perfect product-market fit and brand identity-image alignment: *Beta* wanted to be perceived as a driver of innovation in the Italian market, specifically targeting young customers whose latent need was enjoying Italian food and wine excellences in a new way; on the other hand, the market positively reacted to such a service.

e. **Strategic Responses and Outcomes**

Additionally, in this case, brand visibility and return on investment (ROI) increased dramatically, especially during the Italian lockdown. This represents a solid managerial, marketing, and practical implication, namely, being able to innovate and restructure an SME's business model and channel strategies during and after a crisis event. The CAGR percentages had an exponential boost, thus demonstrating how revenues might benefit from digital marketing activities if coherently designed and implemented in the right market at the right moment.

5.2.3 SMEs' Digitalization and Marketing in the Fintech Industry

Gamma is an Italian SME (100 employees) founded in 2013 and operating in one of the country's most innovative sectors, the fintech industry. Specifically, *Gamma* offers mobile payment services and represents one of the first Italian companies trying to innovate the country's fintech ecosystem. As previously stated in *Beta*'s case description, this is another successful case of Italian SMEs being able to survive the pandemic period and receive a significant investment round exactly in 2020, thus scaling their business model and becoming a benchmark for the market's stakeholders.

a. **Environment**

The fintech industry is *per se* one of the most technology-based and digitalized sectors until the beginning of the I4.0 revolution (Pizzi et al., 2021). Hence, the sustainable competitive advantage seized by Gamma refers to becoming one of the first Italian movers in the fintech ecosystem. A multistakeholder approach characterized *Gamma*'s market entry, which strengthened collaborations and strategic alliances with many key players across industries. As a result, building an open-innovation-based business model able to co-create economic and social value in the targeted market is one of the strategic levers of *Gamma's* success.

b. **Evaluations of the Environment**

Gamma built a very successful partnership with a well-known international e-commerce company, revealing the still-going 'win–win' strategy. On the one hand, *Gamma* gained visibility and, most of all, access to the partner's customer base, which highly appreciated the innovative mobile payment services offered by the Italian SME. This positive reaction of the partner's customer base was largely due to the perfect match between product and market (i.e., product-market fit). On the other hand, the e-commerce company could 'lock in' its customers thanks to *Gamma*'s payment method and all the other lateral services that mainly used a very user-friendly interface both on the website and, particularly, on the app. Again, this business case study stresses the importance of mobile-commerce strategies and apps' importance for a successful digital marketing transition for the company.

c. **Selected Technologies**

Smart and automatic payments require security, privacy, and data management capabilities. Hence, big data analytics (BDA; Rialti et al., 2019) and related stuff are fundamental. Not only are these technologies integrated within the SME's organization but also the way they are accepted and implemented by the company's employees at all levels. This still represents a critical element and barrier to overcome in the Italian SME sector (Kirk & Zollo, 2021).

d. **Selected Implementation Strategy**

Transforming the way people pay was a revolution some years ago, but during and after the pandemic, mobile and intelligent payments are part of our daily activities. *Gamma* was able to create a fintech service very well integrated not only in the Italian stakeholder ecosystem but also in the smartphone app 'world,' being present and perfectly functioning with many of the main existing app stores. Moreover, the critical partnership with the big player in the international e-commerce service industry boosted *Gamma*'s business model scaling. Strengthening collaborations and alliances with companies whose customers might benefit from our services is crucial and allows 'win–win' strategic success.

e. **Strategic Responses and Outcomes**

Gamma's fintech services strongly benefited from the digitalization of the pertinent industry and the specific business model of the SME. The company made customers aware of a new way of making mobile, smart, fast, and easy payment. Therefore, *Gamma* represents a great case of product-market fit, and the economic and financial numbers demonstrate this. Notably, in this case, the pandemic crisis was overcome in a strategic way thanks to financial investors' support and new partnership building, thus emphasizing how open-innovation approaches are fundamental during critical periods.

5.2.4 SMEs' Digitalization and Marketing in Fashion Distribution

Delta is a company based in Florence. It has approximately 50 employees, mainly dealing with direct sales (i.e., sales agent). Initially, Delta started its business operating as a showroom trading fashion shoes. Delta found its business reduced by two concurrent factors. The first is represented by the advent of digital platforms, which allowed buyers to be directly in touch with the producers. The second one was represented by the COVID-19 pandemic, which prevented sales agents from attending fashion shows (Hu et al., 2022). In response to these problems, Delta started its own platform to sell shoes directly to consumers. Benefiting from lower purchase costs, the platform has become highly successful, currently being the third largest Italian-owned fashion product e-tailer.

a. **Environment**

The fashion showroom environment has always been characterized by huge turbulence. Evolving fashion trends and consumers' preferences must be proactive and capable of responding to any possible change. Before the COVID-19 pandemic, digital technologies were used mainly by large brands to be directly in touch with consumers. Such an occurrence was cutting intermediaries such as Delta out of the market. Businesses such as Delta were limiting their use of digital technologies mostly for inventory management and easier or cheaper B2B communication. However, as large brands started to cut intermediaries, technology was deemed by companies such as Delta as a possible response to continue to operate. Indeed, Delta, benefiting from lower purchase costs (due to the greater quantity of items they purchase) than private consumers, could start its e-tailer, selling products from more than one brand online. Its success was determined by the possibility of developing loyalty programs for consumers and by being capable of providing a more customized service to consumers than the brands.

b. **Evaluations of the Environment**

To compete with digital platforms, the only solution identified by Delta's CEO was to develop their digital platform. As it was impossible to be a mono-brand platform (such as any e-commerce from fashion brands), developing a multi-brand platform was deemed the most suitable. Such a choice was considered as coherent with corporate values, as trading multiple brands and making the product reach the right consumers was already part of corporate value. The reduction of B2B sales represented the main problem; however, B2B revenues were almost 150% more than the lost B2B revenues.

c. **Selected Technologies**

Digital platforms and BDA tools were the most relevant technologies employed by Delta. The digital platform is an e-commerce platform with some additional information available for consumers, such as price comparison, items in stocks, and a loyalty program concerning purchases (Marrucci et al., 2022). The key to success for Delta was represented by BDA. Thanks to the possibility of gathering consumer data from their purchases and their social accounts used to log in to the platform, it was possible to produce ad hoc advertising.

d. **Selected Implementation Strategy**

The decision to adopt the technology was top-down. CEO and the most senior marketing manager. The decision to abruptly change how the business operates is something that, according to top management, could have been only their own responsibility. Some of the original sales agents were retrained to manage online platforms; however, it was necessary to hire approximately 30 new employees to manage the company successfully. While the company's two branches (B2B and B2C) operate under the same societal umbrella, the two areas work mostly separately in their daily operations. A strategic decoupling was then pursued to ensure the success of the strategy.

e. **Strategic Responses and Outcomes**

Thanks to the development of the digital platform, Delta survived change. Currently, Delta is among the most profitable companies in its industry. Aside from the B2C business unit, the increase in profits occurred in the B2B business unit. Indeed, data from consumer searches allowed us to forecast future trends better and replenish stocks in the B2B unit with high warehouse rotation index products.

5.2.5 Home Décor and Furniture SMEs Digitalization of Marketing Strategies

Theta is a company producing high-quality furniture based in Verona. It has a long and successful history. The company is recognized as a leading designer of furniture, frequently foreshadowing future market trends in its industry. While technology was initially not perceived as a discriminant in its success, managers soon noticed how thanks to new technologies, it was possible to increase consumer satisfaction while pursuing product innovation solutions.

a. **Environment**

Home décor and high-quality furniture marketing is not highly turbulent. High-net-worth individuals do not suffer from economic downturns like the middle class. In such a regard, maintaining a stable position in the market is an achievable task when a company sells products characterized by a recognizable design. Nevertheless, even this industry is distressed by changing consumer preferences. Such an occurrence is happening due to generational change in consumers. Very few businesses are adapting their offering or how they get in touch with consumers through digital technologies.

b. **Evaluations of the Environment**

In a farsighted way, Theta management scans the environment and perceives the need to change how they interact with younger consumers. Younger consumers want to evaluate the characteristics of a product before their purchase and wish to be assisted during their purchases. There was no direct competitive pressure for Theta, just the desire to interact better with new consumers. Likewise, only a few similar-size competitors were evaluating technological solutions in the industry.

c. **Selected Technologies**

Augmented reality (AR) was the solution identified by Theta marketing managers. AR offered consumers a visualization tool before the finalization of their purchase. Such an instrument, which could be enabled by consumers' download of the Theta mobile phone app, allowed consumers to evaluate how a piece of furniture fits in their homes. First, thanks to AR, consumers could select the proper measures of the item. Second, through chat, they could ask for customized items that fit better about the space a consumer had at home.

d. **Selected Implementation Strategy**

The design department developed the idea to implement AR. Such a department was indeed the one with the greatest technological skills in the company. Initially, designers sought a visualization technique to visualize the developed products in real environments. After that, they suggested implementing it at different levels.

One of the designers was appointed as the team's project manager dedicated to AR implementation in marketing strategies. After several successful tests with loyal consumers, the app was developed and made freely available on AppStore and Google Play. The implementation of AR required an organization-wide strategic renewal process, as it affected development, production, and marketing.

e. **Strategic Responses and Outcomes**

Thanks to AR and the app, increasing the number of consumers registered in the company databases was possible. Many consumers registered to try the app. Likewise, a growing number of younger consumers started to purchase the products from Theta as the overall purchase experience started to be dynamic and different in respect to the competitors' websites (Rialti et al., 2017). As millennials value experience in online purchases more than other consumer cohorts, Theta's solution gave the company a competitive edge over other businesses operating in the same industry.

5.3 Results: The Common Path Toward Digitalization

Overall, our results confirm how the link between environmental adaptation and strategic response to institutional actors and structures is vital for companies' long-term economic and organizational sustainability. We provide a graphical summary of these results in Fig. 5.2, strongly correlated with the institutional perspective outlined previously.

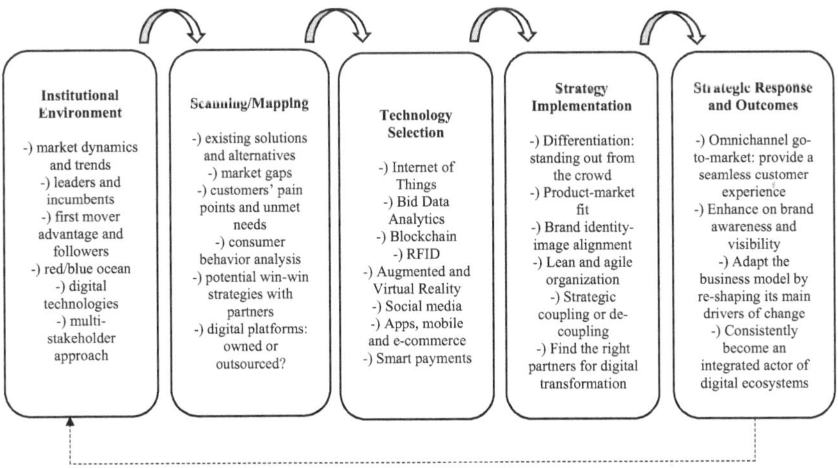

Fig. 5.2 The common path toward digitalization. Source: Authors' Elaboration

The model shown in Fig. 5.2 follows a sequential and iterative process-based view of marketing digitalization. Arrows at the top indicate the step-by-step process marketers should follow according to a 'trial and error' approach (i.e., exploration is essential in innovation). The dotted linkage at the bottom indicates the constant need to monitor and re-elaborate each sub-element in the previous columns to ensure the path toward digitalization is consistent with the company's go-to-market strategy.

Our findings from the interviewees clearly stress that in the first stage of the 'digitalization path,' marketers need to become experts in the environmental opportunity to seize while respecting the institutional dynamics taking place in that specific ecosystem. Being aware of the market players, especially large companies acting as leaders in a market share, is essential to avoid market segments already saturated in competition. As stated in the previous chapters, concepts such as open innovation, multi-stakeholder initiatives, and digital platforms increasingly characterize contemporary markets. Hence, companies must act coherently and realize their institutional role as social actors in that market space.

Next, the second column of the digitalization path takes a whole customer-centric approach by focusing on customers' behavior, unmet expectations, and unfulfilled needs. Companies must understand that digitalization has no sense if customers do not require it. Moreover, product and service innovation must reach the highest degree of personalization possible, thus increasing customer satisfaction and retention. As a result, this second step highlights the importance of designing and creating innovation based on leads, prospects, and customers' needs. Digitalization makes sense when it solves a customer pain point; otherwise, it will result in a negative ROI investment.

The third column indicates the main technologies that emerged from our findings. Here, the most relevant insight is that marketers should choose the appropriate technology for each step of the go-to-market strategy and the customer journey (i.e., awareness, consideration, evaluation and comparison, decision, purchase, post-purchase). The aim is always to improve the customer experience through a better user interface and more personalized touchpoints. The present and future challenge for companies that have a solid offline/physical presence is how to digitalize the customer experience without altering customer satisfaction.

The strategy implementation column indicates the main decision-making processes and strategic thinking companies need to implement, such as differentiation, product-market fit, channel-market fit, identity-image alignment, lean and agile organizational approach, coupling or decoupling, and partnership building. According to our interviewees, these decisions represent the most relevant strategy implementation that might help marketers adopt an effective digitalization path.

Finally, strategic responses and outcomes indicate the modern and future trends of marketing digitalization. Companies can no longer act through a 'silos' approach or propose a multichannel presence that is perceived as a nonintegrated brand experience by customers. Hence, omnichannel initiatives are essential and require a critical rethinking of how companies communicate and interact with stakeholders and customers in a *phygital* way. Digitalization ensures brand visibility and awareness, but marketers need to constantly monitor how brand perception and brand equity evolve during this digital transformation. We need always to assess the brand identity-image alignment and, if necessary, modify the tone of voice, brand presence, offline/online touchpoints, and so on. This requires a new design of the present business model functioning, so marketers need to understand how a change in one of the business model building blocks (i.e., marketing and distribution channels) differently impacts another core element (revenue streams). Finally, companies must be aware that to compete in modern digital ecosystems sustainably, they need to become integrated parts of them. Thus, digitalization requires a deep understanding of the company's institutional social role in the specific market environment.

References

Ardito, L., Petruzzelli, A. M., Panniello, U., & Garavelli, A. C. (2018). Towards Industry 4.0: Mapping digital technologies for supply chain management-marketing integration. *Business Process Management Journal, 25*(2), 323–346.

DiMaggio, P. J., & Powell, W. W. (1991). Introduction. In W. W. Powell & P. J. DiMaggio (Eds.), *The new institutionalism in organizational analysis* (pp. 1–38). University of Chicago Press.

Faraoni, M., Rialti, R., & Zollo, L. (2018). How to foster wine online purchasing behavior? Empirical evidences from Italy. In: *2018 global marketing conference at Tokyo* (pp. 1419–1419).

Gervasi, D., Faldetta, G., & Zollo, L. (2022). How to prevent incivility from women employees? The role of psychological contract violation, aggressive reciprocal attitude and conscientiousness. *International Journal of Manpower*. https://doi.org/10.1108/IJM-06-2021-0340

Gervasi, D., Faldetta, G., Zollo, L., & Lombardi, S. (2022). Does TMX affect instigated incivility? The role of negative reciprocity and psychological contract violation. *Management Decision, 60*(11), 3066–3085.

Hu, L., Filieri, R., Acikgoz, F., Zollo, L., & Rialti, R. (2022). The effect of utilitarian and hedonic motivations on mobile shopping outcomes. A cross-cultural analysis. *International Journal of Consumer Studies*. https://doi.org/10.1111/ijcs.12868

Kirk, N. H., & Zollo, L. (2021). *European Venture Toolbox: The path for SMEs to grasp and defend opportunities*. Emerald Group Publishing.

Krings, W., Palmer, R., & Inversini, A. (2021). Industrial marketing management digital media optimization for B2B marketing. *Industrial Marketing Management, 93*, 174–186.

Marrucci, A., Rialti, R., Donvito, R., & Syed, F. U. (2022). "Connected we stand, disconnected we fall". Analyzing the importance of digital platforms in transnational supply chain management. *International Journal of Emerging Markets* (ahead-of-print).

McDermott, A. M., Fitzgerald, L., & Buchanan, D. A. (2013). Beyond acceptance and resistance: Entrepreneurial change agency responses in policy implementation. *British Journal of Management, 24*, S93–S115.

Pizzi, S., Corbo, L., & Caputo, A. (2021). Fintech and SMEs sustainable business models: Reflections and considerations for a circular economy. *Journal of Cleaner Production, 281*, 125217. https://doi.org/10.1016/j.jclepro.2020.125217

Ranfagni, S., Faraoni, M., Zollo, L., & Vannucci, V. (2021). Combining online market research methods for investigating brand alignment: The case of Nespresso. *British Food Journal, 123*(13), 37–58.

Rialti, R., Marzi, G., Caputo, A., & Mayah, K. A. (2020). Achieving strategic flexibility in the era of big data: The importance of knowledge management and ambidexterity. *Management Decision, 58*(8), 1585–1600.

Rialti, R., Marzi, G., Ciappei, C., & Busso, D. (2019). Big data and dynamic capabilities: A bibliometric analysis and systematic literature review. *Management Decision*. https://doi.org/10.1108/MD-07-2018-0821

Rialti, R., Zollo, L., Pellegrini, M. M., & Ciappei, C. (2017). Exploring the antecedents of brand loyalty and electronic word of mouth in social-media-based brand communities: Do gender differences matter? *Journal of Global Marketing, 30*(3), 147–160.

Scott, W. R. (2008). *Institutions and organizations: Ideas and interests*. Sage Publications.

Scuotto, V., Nicotra, M., Del Giudice, M., Krueger, N., & Gregori, G. L. (2021). A microfoundational perspective on SMEs' growth in the digital transformation era. *Journal of Business Research, 129*, 382–392.

Vijayakumar, D. S. (2020). Digital twin in consumer choice modeling. *Advances in Computers, 117*(1), 265–284.

Wang, X., Wang, Y., Tao, F., & Liu, A. (2021). New paradigm of data-driven smart customisation through digital twin. *Journal of Manufacturing Systems, 58*, 270–280.

Yang, Z., & Su, C. (2014). Institutional theory in business marketing: A conceptual framework and future directions. *Industrial Marketing Management, 43*(5), 721–725.

Zollo, L., Pellegrini, M. M., Faldetta, G., & Rialti, R. (2022). How to combine multiple identities and gaining stakeholders legitimacy in hybrid organizations? An organizational design response. *Journal of Management and Governance*. https://doi.org/10.1007/s10997-022-09644-7

6

How Can Managers Transform SME Marketing Strategies in a 4.0 Fashion?

6.1 SME 4.0 Marketing Transformation

The insights that emerged from our in-depth qualitative analysis of the business case study have been summarized in the following framework (see Fig. 6.1), which might be interpreted as an iterative practical step-by-step checklist that SMEs' marketers could follow to implement a digital transformation of their business activities.

We build on Kirk and Zollo's (2021, p. 48) model—the Entrepreneurial Journey Framework—to identify iteratively and dynamically the strategic tools (i.e., building blocks of the model) SMEs should put into practice for surviving a digital transformation currently, with a specific focus on business marketing.

In the first stage, SMEs must be aware of the *status quo* of their industry regarding the main technological trends as well as stakeholders and competitors 'altering' the game's rules. History in business plays a crucial role by clearly showing how companies that could not anticipate disruptive changes and new market equilibria were forced to fail or change businesses (i.e., Blockbuster vs. Netflix, Nokia vs. Apple, iTunes vs. Spotify, etc.). Moreover, as emerged clearly from the analyzed business cases, it

R. Rialti, L. Zollo, *Digital Transformation of SME Marketing Strategies*,
https://doi.org/10.1007/978-3-031-33646-1_6

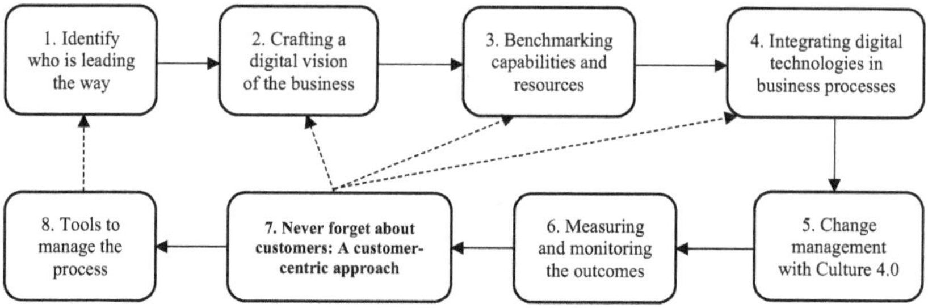

Fig. 6.1 A practical checklist for SMEs' digital transformation. Notes: ⟶ Arrows indicate the sequential logic to be followed across the building blocks of the checklist model. ----▸ Dotted arrows indicate the feedback loop nature of the model, stressing the 'trial-and-error' approach marketers must adopt to go back and forth continuously to accomplish a customer-centric digital transformation of their business. Source: Authors' elaboration

becomes crucial for SME marketers to identify potential partners, allies, or collaborators prone to develop strategic alliances that could foster digital transformation success. Let us consider, for example, designing a digital twin strategy to foresee customers' reactions after the introduction of a specific product: if the SME has neither the financial possibility nor the technological capability to implement this digital process, it is fundamental to understand whom to interact and collaborate with in the institutional environment.

After identifying the market, assessing industry characteristics, and individuating potential supporting partners and policies, SME entrepreneurs, managers, and marketers need to start turning their traditional, conventional mindset into a new digital technology-oriented mindset. Hence, they need to focus on how it can improve traditional ways of running the business through the help of digital technologies. Recrafting business model 'architecture' (Amit & Zott, 2015) plays a key role: digital transition should encompass all four steps of business modeling crafting, such as (1) new *goals* to capture socioeconomic and environmental value—scouting and then solving new customers' pain points and unfulfilled expectations levering digital opportunities; (2) new *templates* of large players in the industry and specific market—a deep understanding of the way incumbents successfully exploited new technology implementation to gain market share; (3) new *stakeholder* activities and initiatives—as stressed before, SMEs alone cannot survive modern markets that are increasingly unpredictable and dynamic, which is why creating a solid and sustainable network of partnerships with stakeholders is crucial; and (4) *environmental* constraints and opportunities—consistent with the institutional logic stressed before, SMEs must adapt their business model transformation in line with the market's trends by respecting the institutional agents' requirements and expectations. Our in-depth case study demonstrates these are among the key drivers of success, especially as reported by SMEs' managers and founders.

SMEs should then consistently align scouted market opportunities with their available resources (human, tangible, and intangible) and capabilities. As stressed multiple times in the present work and specifically in the qualitative methodology, if marketers want to exploit the digital transition of their branding, channel, advertising, and so on activities, a cultural change and evolution is needed. New technologies allow several advantages and opportunities, especially in reaching new targeted customer segments and better exploring their behavioral intentions. Still, digitalization also requires a deep knowledge (both hard skills and soft skills) of these new technologies. Hence, the digital transitioning of a business must go hand in hand with a cultural change—as will be presented later—and an upskilling of the SME's personnel.

Now SMEs have identified the right technologies and the required skillsets, the most delicate building block for SMEs wishing to digitalize occurs. This phase is particularly complex because it requires a careful cost-benefit analysis (CBA) to assess how and when to integrate new digital tools into each element of the company's business model. Regarding 'how', SME managers need to integrate new technologies coherently to innovate—but not disintegrate—the traditional mechanisms used to create value. Concerning the 'when', SMEs need time management; in other words, timing is essential to propose a new image, for example, toward their market and stakeholders, to be perceived as the same company but in a redesigned, better-updated version. The aim is usually twofold; on the one hand, SMEs must create better value for their customers (i.e., gaining 'legitimacy' from an institutional theory perspective), and on the other hand, this has to be pursued concerning a profit-and-loss positive bottom line. A deep understanding of motivations—both psychological and sociological—leading customers to adopt new tech-based products might be a strategic approach to positioning SMEs' products and services correctly (Hu et al., 2022). Without such an understanding, our analyzed business cases would not have survived the pandemic crisis.

Next, one of the most prominent elements affecting SMEs' business model when transitioning toward the digital landscape refers to culture and the resulting organizational behavior (Jamali et al., 2020). Corporate culture is a strategic means through which entrepreneurs and founders express, manifest, and communicate their SMEs' identity, made of values, principles, history, and entrepreneurial passion (Zollo, Rialti et al., 2021). Unfortunately, resistance to change represents a main barrier and obstacle for SMEs, especially micro and small companies rooted in a conventional approach toward entrepreneurship (Kirk & Zollo, 2021). As emerged from the empirical findings, SMEs need to change their strategic vision dynamically and, in turn, mission to survive during critical eras such as the pandemic. From this perspective, being able to exploit digital transformation opportunities effectively brings paramount benefits to companies' performance, allowing entrepreneurs to rethink and redesign their traditional way of doing business.

The 'monitoring and measuring' building block emphasizes the necessity to integrate in every step of the SME's supply chain instruments—such as interactive and dynamic dashboards—in order to constantly monitor and evaluate the company's performance. KPIs assume a critical and essential role, as previously seen when talking about digital marketing KPIs.

The framework's second to last element stresses this chapter's primary underlying rationale: SMEs willing to survive a digital transformation successfully must follow and adopt a customer-centric approach. Scholars agree on this (Kirk & Zollo, 2021) by stating that the transition is not technological-oriented but focused on addressing targeted customers' new—sometimes latent—needs and expectations. As our qualitative analysis demonstrates, it is not a digital transition *per se*, but it must be a purposeful economic, cultural, and organizational change to create more value. For each investment an SME makes, managers and marketers should ask themselves, 'What type of value are we creating for our customers?'. If no clear answer is provided, then it is likely that the SME will suffer from negative ROI performance, meaning that the investment in digital transformation will not be positively correlated with metrics related to revenues or profits. As shown in the model (see Fig. 6.1), this building block is linked to several other elements of the checklist, mainly because it is the core vital element able to maintain the necessary functioning of the digital transition.

Finally, the building block labeled 'tools to manage the process' refers to the practical implementation of all the strategies previously discussed. The pertinent section in the following will analyze in detail all the appropriate tools SMEs might use to successfully overcome the transition. However, the linkage between this final building block and the first one, 'identify who is leading the way', stresses how managers and marketers need constant monitoring of the market situation to realize and understand what the most strategic tools are to be implemented for an efficient and effective strategy. Again, as our findings demonstrate, it is not the tool *per se* that assumes relevance but how it is used and for what purpose.

6.1.1 Identify Who Is Leading the Way

Before implementing any digital technology, SMEs must identify who is leading the way in the industry. Orienting amid the plethora of existing digital technologies is extremely difficult; similarly, it may pose unprecedented challenges. 'Which technology may work in your case?', 'Why is it going to work?', and 'How is it going to work?' are three questions whose answer is difficult to identify without any case or best practice to observe.

Coherently, observing the best in the class may provide some relevant insights to decide which technology may be helpful and to understand which may be the principal effects of its implementation (Matt et al., 2015).

Marketers of SMEs need to identify the best one among your competitors to comprehend what it is doing. Specifically, suppose you are a small company in need of expanding your customer base. In that case, a good solution may be looking at competitors who have already implemented and owned e-commerce platforms or are exploiting existing e-commerce websites. From this perspective, it may be essential to identify the ones having the best performance and why their strategies are working or not.

On the other hand, if you are working for a big player, you may need to identify who is already looking into the future. Indeed, if one of your principal competitors is implementing systems to increase supply chain management efficiency, you may need to understand why it is implementing such technologies. Similarly, it would be best if you focused on any actions from competitors that could potentially harm your market share. Hence, you will need to observe who is trying to implement any technology capable of increasing online or in-store sales. This is the only way to respond to any eventual change.

Managers must always consider that a universal best way to lead to a successful digital transformation has yet to be created. A technological solution may generate extra revenues for an SME but may prove ineffective in another case. Its peculiarities characterize any SME. Similarly, each company has its different customer base, which may or may not appreciate a new technology. Moving from this, we will present a comprehensive schedule to implement digital transformation. Specifically, the proposed schedule will be a framework that may be followed by any SME regardless of its scale or its context of operation (Zhu et al., 2006). Accordingly, the first phase is to observe who already succeeded in implementing a technology or who is generating the most revenues from a digital technology.

6.1.2 Making the Case for Digital Transformation: Crafting the Vision Within Your Business

As assessed in the first chapter, it is fundamental for managers trying to successfully implement a digital technology to make the case for digital transformation. Accordingly, this is the second phase of any digital transformation process after observing competitors' strategies (Berman, 2012).

Coherently, the appropriate first act a manager must do in this perspective is to make everyone understand the need for digital technology. A very good way of doing so may be represented by an explanation to everyone involved in the business that the traditional methods the company is run need to be updated. Then, everyone should understand how digital technologies are changing the competitive landscape. In detail, a good leader should try to describe how the business will only survive the emerging competition with transformation, which is the essence of making the case. To do so, the lender may decide to bring to the table what competitors are doing and why such actions will damage their business. For example, explaining to other people within the organization that competitors' e-commerce implementation may potentially erode our business's market share will be extremely useful. In a similar fashion, there is a need to explain how automatic machines may reduce the need for some annoying or repetitive manual tasks that could help workers (such as people working in warehouses) reduce some difficulties present in their jobs. Finally, it may be necessary to explain to employees that new in-store technologies may be required to improve customers' experience and to increase the quantity of sales, which is particularly true in the case competitors have already implemented new technologies such as VR or AR capable of improving customers' perceptions of the store and the products.

Thus, anyone in charge of a digital transformation must make the case or explain why the business needs to transform. Only in this way will employees listen to him/her. Making everyone perceive the urgency of the transformation is, therefore, fundamental. Indeed, if people fear that the company they work for may go under if it does not transform, then this will help them accept the change. However, explaining why the business is transforming is one of many things managers should do. They should also explain how the industry is changing. Making the case stronger is necessary to provide people with a detailed plan of what will change (Westerman et al., 2014b). Therefore, in our context, which digital technology will be implemented, and what are the expected outcomes?

As it may be possible to imagine, there may need to be more than making the case to motivate everyone involved in the organization. It is also important to spend time crafting the vision of digital transformation within the business. As most readers already know, the vision is a form of commonly shared mental projection that concerns how the company will be in the future. It is then an ensemble of goals, objectives, steps that people need to trust to understand properly why the business is changing. Consequently, as digital technology implementation may change the way the business will be in the future, the need to craft a vision to drive digital transformation emerges.

Specifically, digital transformation leaders will need to create a vision concerning how the business will work after implementing new digital technologies. Therefore, leaders need to try to create a sort of 'statement' including the following contents:

1. How will the business be in the future?
2. How it will be like working for the digitally transformed business?
3. The effects of digital technologies on the ways the business will run its internal operations and processes.
4. The effects of digital technologies on the ways the business will be in touch with customers.
5. How digital technologies will allow the business to be more competitive?
6. How digital technologies will create value?
7. Why are digital technologies necessary for the survival of businesses in the digital era?

Such a statement, as previously assessed, will be fundamental. In fact, people are usually more motivated if they can perceive the existence of a vision to follow if they will be part of the digital transformation.

6.1.3 Benchmarking Current Capabilities and Defying Resource Requirements

The moment digital transformation leaders/leaders have transmitted their vision about the digital future of the business, then they will have to understand which kind of capabilities and resources they will need to transform their business successfully.

Therefore, during the initial planning of digital transformation, they need to make a list of which intangible capabilities and which tangible resources are required to proceed.

Then, to do so, any digital transformation leader needs to (1) be aware of the generically necessary capabilities and resources to digitally transform, (2) benchmark existing capabilities and resources with the required ones, and (3) try to develop missing capabilities and to acquire missing resources. These are discussed in detail in the following paragraphs.

i. **Identifying the Capabilities and Resources Usually Needed to Implement a Digital Transformation**

Extant research has identified two main kinds of capabilities and one main kind of resource usually necessary for implementing digital transformation in any business.

Regarding capabilities for digital transformation, managerial capabilities and employees' capabilities concerning digital technologies are fundamental. These are managers' capabilities necessary to understand digital technology. Specifically, managerial abilities regard managers' capability to understand the underlying mechanism of digital technology, to understand the specific effects of implementing a digital technology, and to comprehend at least the basics of how to use the digital technology. If the manager is endowed with such capabilities, they will also be able to identify and select the most suitable technology for business objectives (Matt et al., 2015). Similarly, such specific capabilities are essential because they may enable managers to determine how to implement the technology and how to evaluate employees' capabilities and resource adequateness.

Next, employees' capabilities are a set of capabilities concerning employees' practical skills in the use of digital technologies. Specifically, such capabilities regard how confidently employees may use a digital technology based on how much they have been trained. Employees' capabilities are fundamental for two reasons. First, employees' capabilities matter, as employees confident in digital technologies will not oppose the implementation of new tools. Second, suppose employees are already skilled in digital technologies' use. In that case, they will not commit many common mistakes during early use of technologies, which will then be 100% usable in the very early stages of their implementation (Westerman et al., 2014b).

Finally, regarding the most necessary resource, it was observed that the most important 'resource' is usually a proper technological infrastructure or at least an infrastructure that may be updated time by time according to the new emerging technological requirements/standards. A flexible technological infrastructure is then the principal resource that is needed to foster any digital transformation. In detail, an infrastructure may be suitable to support a digital transformation process if it is already based on databases, servers, networked computers, and machines that may support new technologies emerging over time. However, such an architecture should also not be oversized or too costly to maintain if the need to reduce the size of digital operations appears in the future. Accordingly, in the current digital environment, a wise solution to create a flexible infrastructure capable of being used in any situation is represented by the use of cloud computing. A business may implement a basic adaptable and flexible infrastructure without excessive computation capacity and ask a cloud computing provider to analyze extra data flows over time. It emerges then how cloud computing is a form of data analysis outsourcing. The existing technological infrastructure may be considered a strategically important resource only if it allows the exchange of significant information over time. Thus, it should be linked to a high-speed internet network (Rialti, Marzi et al., 2018; Rialti et al., 2019).

As it is possible to understand, the digital transformation leader should be aware of such necessary factors. Indeed, only if he/she is aware of them will they be able to benchmark the existing capabilities and resources with those necessary to make the transformation work.

ii. **Benchmarking Existing Capabilities and Resources with the Required Ones**

As soon as leaders know that a digital transformation needs to be implemented and know about the effects of digital transformation and the capabilities and resources generically required to transform the business properly, the time for benchmarking existing capabilities and help with the required ones has come.

In effect, before starting any operative phase, the leader must confront what they have at disposition with the effective capabilities and resources needed to complete the digital transformation successfully.

Accordingly, a good solution may be represented by conducting interviews or surveys with managers and employees to assess their degree of confidence toward new technologies. Additionally, a qualitative evaluation of effective skills (i.e., with tests or assessments) could be something that deserves to be considered by digital transformation leaders. What should emerge from these analyses, in this perspective, is the distance between the current capabilities and the required ones. As an example, it should emerge which kind of digital technology skills managers and employees need to be included in the business (Caputo et al., 2016; Rialti et al., 2019).

Regarding infrastructure, an assessment by technicians may be fundamental. Thus, testing the computing capability and data transfer speed of existing systems could be useful. In the case of SMEs, for example, if the digital transformation project involves the implementation of e-commerce data storage, infrastructural capabilities may need to be added. Thus, the digital transformation leader will need to consider how to increase the storage capabilities of the business to collect new data emerging from online transactions. Otherwise, if the project is about the implementation of VR or AR, it may be fundamental to evaluate whether the existing internet speed or computation capacity of systems are sufficient to make the new systems run.

iii. **Developing Missing Capabilities or Acquiring Missing Resources**

Finally, the digital transformation leader must develop a plan to acquire the missing capabilities or resources. Therefore, training plans and educational courses concerning digital skills or programs to influence managers' and employees' perceptions of digital technologies emerged.

Similarly, the need to find the right provider of systems to bear the implementation of a new technology became pressing at this moment. Only a provider who knows exactly how to implement the required strategies may ensure the desired outcomes.

In this context, the need for another resource also emerges, namely, money. Digital transformation could, in fact, be an extremely costly process. Money is fundamental to support the development of all capabilities and acquiring resources for digital technologies.

6.1.4 Integrating New Digital Technologies Into Current Systems and Processes

In theory, a digital transformation leader may be able to lead a successful digital transformation after the identification of the right technology, the assessment of the gaps existing regarding resources and capabilities, and the effective development of a plan. However, as with any business transformation/evolution, a shift toward digital technology will not occur overnight. Businesses are, in fact, complex systems kept together by very difficult micro-mechanisms based on routines, existing tools/systems, and recurring processes. Hence, new digital technologies may represent factors disrupting day-to-day operations. Digital transformation leaders will also need to consider how to integrate new digital technologies into existing systems and processes from a technical point of view (Tallon & Pinsonneault, 2011). This phase is crucial in any digital transformation process for several reasons.

First, if a digital transformation leader can instate new technologies into existing processes and systems, it may save money and realization time. On the one hand, the existence of an architecture to implement the new technology may prevent additional expenditure for digital transformation. Existing systems that share additional data from new technologies represent an excellent ground to build your new technologies. On the other hand, the existence of some infrastructure may surely save time. Specifically, in such cases, there is no need to start the construction of the architecture from scratch (Rialti, Marzi et al., 2018).

Second, if it is possible to exploit an existing system, it will be possible to leverage existing managers' and employees' skills concerning using the techniques. Thus, it will allow the leader of digital transformation to improve the efficiency of the whole change. Usually, in a digital transformation process, a considerable amount of time is dedicated to retraining all the workforce that will have to deal with digital technologies. As an example, consider the significant impact of the shift from traditional advertising channels to social media. For another example, imagine all the retraining that is necessary to make the workforce of a physical store capable of using AR, VR, or any other automatic technology (Pizzi et al., 2019). This enforces the need to use something already existing, at least in part, so that the people in your company will use the technology faster and better. In fact, the workforce usually does not reject new technological tools based on existing infrastructures or IT systems. In fact, such kinds of new technologies will be perceived by everyone in the organization as just an extension of something already in place. Thus, they will be confident of their ability to use them and of their outcomes.

Third, if a manager chooses to implement a new technology, moving from something already existing, they will be safer about the potential outcomes. If at least some components of digital technology have already been tested because of previous applications, the potential consequences of implementing a new technology will be more specific (Tallon & Pinsonneault, 2011). Similarly, most potential problems that may emerge have probably already been observed in the past, and someone already knows the solution.

To do that, some checks need to be done. First, the digital transformation leader will need to assess the capacity of existing IT infrastructure to support a new technology. IT infrastructure storage capacity, data transmission capability, and effective multiple-device usability must be observed. For instance, an IT system based on very outdated components may not be able to sustain the data flows necessary in the significant data era.

After benchmarking between existing systems' capabilities and the required capabilities, how to proceed forward needs to be decided next. At this point, it may be necessary to evaluate whether the money needed to build a new technology on existing systems is worth the cost. If the price is coherent with expectations, managers should select the people who made the original system, and they will be more confident in the modifications required to instate the new technology on existing IT architecture.

6.1.5 Handling Change Management by Managing Culture

Every business is characterized by its own culture and subcultures. Accordingly, each business is characterized by values and behaviors that can shape the existing sociocultural environment, how people interact, and resistance to any eventual change.

As it is possible to understand, culture is something that is related to recurring routines and existing ways of completing activities and tasks. From this perspective, it was widely observed in all the fields of managerial literature that transformation leaders should always take culture into account if the need to transform some process within the business emerges. Transformation leaders and managers should, in fact, first be aware of how things work in a company. Then, they should constantly observe how people deal with a problem and how usual everyone runs processes. Ultimately, they should be able to understand correctly why these processes are run in this way. When they are fully aware of what is going on, they can finally think about how to change the business. Clearly, the first act of digital transformation leaders and managers should include diffusing the benefits of the new idea. The communication of the vision is fundamental to make everyone understand what will change and why it will change (Kane et al., 2015). However, due to culture's importance, the focus on communicating the vision may not be sufficient. Indeed, the explanation of 'how' something is going to change becomes fundamental. To avoid resistance to change, managers should certainly explain to everyone affected by the transformation process that they could continue to work as usual if they will be available to adapt to the use of different tools or different technologies. Coherently, leaders and managers should be able to communicate that life within the business will continue as always.

Digital transformation endeavors present no exception in this perspective. Then, an excellent way to do that is to explain to everyone that some 'old fashioned' tasks will be easier to complete due to digital transformation. By using digital tools, some repetitive manual tasks may be completed faster and better with the help of automatic machines. No employees should feel left behind because of digital transformation.

Specifically, no one should perceive the risk of losing their job due to digital transformation. Leaders should try to avoid firing someone, as digital transformation has suddenly made their job obsolete. Understandably, some cuts may be necessary due to the transformation. Still, leaders and managers should be able to properly explain that those cuts were not a direct consequence of digital transformation (Wamba & Mishra, 2017). Indeed, suppose people feel that their jobs are threatened by digital transformation, or they perceive that adapting to the new digital business will be too difficult. In that case, they will react negatively by trying to prevent change.

Culture may be a very good instrument to make the digital transformation smoother. For instance, if digital transformation leaders have identified the central values, behaviors, and routines coexisting within the business, they may develop strategies capable of using culture as a boost. In fact, digital transformation leaders and managers could decide to instate new processes on existing behaviors and routines, thus making people feel involved in the decision processes. Indeed, a change allowing people to continue to follow their routines at work will be accepted more straightforwardly by everyone. Therefore, leveraging an existing culture is one of the most significant challenges for any change manager, but if he/she can do so, then resistance will be minimal, and costs will be lower.

6.1.6 Measuring the Outcomes

The final challenge for any digital transformation leader is represented by evaluating the digital transformation process and its outcomes. Such a phase is particularly tricky, as any leader or manager may be prone to free-riding behavior; thus, they may be inclined to report greater achievements rather than writing the effectively accomplished ones. This is particularly true if they are an external professional hired to manage the digital transformation. Regardless, internal managers may also try to show the managing directors, partners, or shareholders better results than the ones effectively achieved. Building on these premises, a series of best practices to measure digital transformation outcomes is needed.

However, how can a digital transformation process be evaluated? Anecdotal evidence from completed digital transformation evaluation procedures may help us.

First, it is necessary to benchmark what has been implemented with respect to the initial objectives and the original vision of digital transformation. Such control is probably the most objective; in fact, vision is not objectively measurable; it is just an ideal representation in managers' and shareholders' minds. Then, to complete such an evaluation, it is necessary to consider the original scope of the digital transformation, how it should have influenced existing procedures and the way of doing work, and how much it has effectively affected the business. Hence, such an evaluation will consist of a comparison between an idealized situation and an actual situation. It will be observed whether the digital transformation process was at least partially able to meet the expectations in managers' minds.

Currently, such an evaluation of the matching between vision and reality is performed, and then a second evaluation may be performed (www.technation.com). Indeed, after preliminary assessing the correspondence between vision and reality, it is necessary to assess the capabilities obtained due to the digital transformation. Such an evaluation may be articulated into two different phases. First, it is necessary to consider the skills that employees have developed due to retraining and the daily use of new technological tools. In fact, if the workforce has either yet to learn any lesson from implementing new technologies or people refuse to develop personal abilities to use technologies, even the best new technology will not be useful in the future. For example, an SME may adopt the best AR system in its stores, but if the workforce cannot make it work, it will not have any practical utility. Then, attention should be given to the assessment of the adequateness of the technological infrastructure. Specifically, the person in charge of the evaluation should consider whether the implemented infrastructure is able to reach the prefixed scopes.

As it is possible to understand, the two evaluations are particularly challenging from a technical standpoint. Indeed, the evaluation of the capabilities of personnel requires human resource capability assessments. For example, simulations regarding the ability to use a technology or tests to evaluate the level of theoretical expertise may be fundamental. Instead, of what concerns the evaluation of technological infrastructure, the assessment requires engineers and systems experts capable of evaluating the failure rate of the systems. Such technicians may evaluate the appropriateness of a procedure in terms of data flows, data storage, and effectiveness in its functions and potential problems that may emerge using informatic engineering methodologies.

Another criterion that can be used to evaluate the success of a digital transformation is the evaluation of the costs of the endeavor. Accordingly, most change management projects are frequently plagued by cost overruns and delays, and digital transformations are commonly affected by the same problems. Hence, it is impossible to deem a project successful if it costs ten times the expected cost. The total expenditures, including hidden or sunk costs, should also be considered for this. A digital transformation costing ten times the sum paid by a competitor but having the same effects may, in fact, not be considered adequately executed. Such a kind of evaluation is then related to the efficacy of the implementation.

Finally, the last evaluation that should be done after digital transformation is related to the assessment of the impact of digital transformation on existing processes. This specific evaluation is an evaluation of the effectiveness of the implementation. Indeed, in the case of the implementation of new technologies, it is necessary for managers to objectively assess whether such technologies are effectively capable of completing the hypothesized tasks. During this ex-post evaluation, managers observe whether the desired effect of digital transformation has emerged. As it is possible to imagine, such a final evaluation involves the direct observation of the output of the implementation of each technology. From this perspective, listening to customers' feedback is an excellent solution to conduct this evaluation.

6.1.7 Don't Forget About Customers

As assessed in the previous paragraph, an excellent way to evaluate the success of a digital transformation is to evaluate customer feedback. For SMEs, most of the new technologies are implanted to increase the level of service for customers. Consequently, a digital transformation process cannot be considered a success simply by looking at the value it may create; it is, in fact, necessary to also consider how digital transformation has affected customers' perceptions. If customers are satisfied with the improvement digital technologies bring to their shopping experience, the digital transformation can be deemed successful.

However, what are the focal points of this evaluation of the effects on customers?

i. **Customer Trust and Satisfaction**

SMEs should always monitor the level of customers' trust and satisfaction. Confidence and satisfaction are related to customers' intention to select a company over another and to customers' intention to repurchase products eventually. Traditionally, regarding physical stores, trust, and satisfaction are derived jointly from the ability of the salesforce to assist customers properly and from the store environment (Setia et al., 2013).

However, after a digital transformation, some new factors need to be considered if there is a need to evaluate how trust and satisfaction increase. Digital technologies may, in fact, be drivers of trust and satisfaction. Specifically, if digital technologies improve the in-store atmosphere as perceived by customers, their satisfaction will also increase. Similarly, if digital technologies can protect customers' data, their trust toward the SME may increase (Morey et al., 2015). Then, it is fundamental to monitor the effect of digital technologies on confidence and satisfaction based on customers' opinion pools. If trust and satisfaction decrease due to digital transformation, some changes will, in fact, be necessary.

ii. **Customers' Experience**

Customers' experience may refer either to customers' in-store experience or customers' online experience. The first one refers to customers' experience during their purchases in a physical store. The second one regards customers' experience during their purchases while using an online platform. Usually, previous studies have identified experience as one of the most relevant factors of customer loyalty toward a specific company (Parise et al., 2016). Indeed, a customer with a positive purchase experience will probably be more prone to revisit the same store/website and recommend it to peers.

Customers' in-store experience may derive from several different factors, such as the treatment that customers received in the store, availability of the desired products, and the possibility of discussing with the salesforce about the quality of products. On the other hand, online experience derives from website characteristics and usability, availability of products, ability to meet the expected delivery time, and perceived safeness of payment methods.

As it is possible to imagine, new digital technologies' implementation may influence customers' overall experience, both in regard to the in-store experience and online experience. Indeed, about in-store experience, new digital technologies may make it easier for customers to find a product, help them to look for customized promotions, improve their payment methods, and improve how they select products (i.e., by using AR or VR). Like the online experience, digital technologies may improve customers' experience, as they can help e-tailers tailor customized offerings and promotions (i.e., due to big data analytics), offer customers the possibility to customize a product, and improve the safety of payments.

Accordingly, one of the consequences of digital transformation should be improving both customers' in-store experience and online experience.

iii. **Customers' Service and Customer Relationship Management**

With the implementation of digital technologies, SMEs may offer customers increased service. Digital technologies are, in fact, touchpoints capable of allowing a company to better listen and communicate with customers. Therefore, in the current times, an SME may know better than ever what customers need, what they expect in-store or during a purchase on an online platform, and what they appreciate or do not appreciate during their experience. Moving from the possibility of better understanding customers' needs, it is possible to understand how a better service can be offered to customers. As an example, using touchscreens or in-store technologies, customers may give SMEs real-time feedback about the in-store environment, product placement, and salespersons' behavior. Accordingly, the SME may take corrective actions to improve the next visit. Instead, regarding online environments, using data about navigation and purchases that a company may collect, the marketer may provide suggestions about products to customers or eventually provide information about payment methods.

Apart from that, as it is possible to imagine, new touchpoints to communicate with customers may improve SME customer relationship management (CRM). The essence of CRM is, in fact, in the control of the relationship with customers with the help of interactions aimed at increasing customers' trust and satisfaction over time. For example, good CRM strategies can increase customers' intention to return to a specific store or repurchase a product online. Customers targeted by CRM strategies, additionally, are more prone to provide vital feedback to SMEs. Finally, because of CRM strategies, customers are usually prone to diffuse positive word-of-mouth about a company (Quinton, 2013).

iv. **Customers' Engagement and Loyalty**

A customer is engaged if they are in a very fond relationship with an SME. Engaged customers usually perceive their relationship with an SME as an extremely intimate bond. Engaged customers expect more from the company than customers who need more engagement. However, because of such a bond, they are more prone to again visit the SME's store and look for the company's stores instead of the competitors' stores. They will advocate for the SME even amidst difficulties. Engaged customers represent an extremely relevant competitive advantage (Gambetti & Graffigna, 2010). Customers' engagement is extremely related to customer loyalty, which may be defined as the extent to which customers are devoted to an SME and its products.

Digital technologies can also influence customers' engagement and loyalty. Satisfaction and trust, which are the most relevant antecedents of engagement and loyalty, may be affected by digital technology implementation (Anderson & Srinivasan, 2003). Specifically, it may be assumed that due to digital technologies, an SME may be more in touch with customers, be more capable of developing a bond with him/her, and influence customers' perceptions.

v. **Customer Centricity**

Because of the improved CRM strategies, which may increase customers' trust, satisfaction, and experience, customers' centricity will increase. Then, digital technology implementation may bring the customer to the center of any company's strategies (Liang & Tanniru, 2006).

6.1.8 Tools to Manage the Process

Focusing only on skills and capabilities necessary for digital transformations may prove a huge mistake for any manager. Indeed, while skills and capabilities are fundamental for any digital transformation, the need for tools to improve digital transformation management is evident to anyone that has ever tried to transform a business digitally. Tools, accordingly, may contribute to digital transformation in two ways: (1) first, they may be a technology required to implement new systems; (2) second, they may help managers observe the performance of the digital transformation process.

Regarding the tools necessary to instate new digital technologies, the most common ones are the Internet of Things (IoT), artificial intelligence (AI) and machine learning-capable systems, big data capable infrastructures, big data processing tools, and extensive data storage systems (i.e., cloud-based storage systems such as data lakes). As you may remember, the importance of these tools (or digital technologies) was widely discussed in previous chapters. It is always important to remember their role in digital transformation. With them, indeed, it is possible to think about digital transformation. Accordingly, in their absence, it will not be possible to instate new technologies on existing ones, and digital transformation will cost the company too much money.

Instead, we still need to discuss important tools that may help managers monitor digital transformation advances. Digital transformation, like any process aiming at transforming a business, should be monitored over time to control how the whole process goes and how far the business is from the desired outcome. As it is possible to imagine, these tools are frequently technologies fundamental in enabling control mechanisms. For instance, digital transformation managers and leaders have pointed out several tools that may work (www.apmdigest.com), namely:

i. **Application Performance Management Technologies (APM)**

APM technologies are a typology of tools that may be used to monitor the performance of applications (apps) that customers may download on their devices. Such tools can collect data about customers' usage of an online application. Data such as usage time, most used function, touches, scrolls, internal navigation, and failure (crash) rates are collected over time. Such tools also need to be capable of analyzing data and providing insights to analysts. From this perspective, it was pointed out how they should embed data analytics capabilities, transaction analytics, and agent code instrumentation (i.e., being accessible by business agents and programmers capable of writing in informatics languages). The main advantages related to these tools derive from the possibility of knowing how customers using an app are reacting to change over time and form the chance to tell if newly developed apps are working as expected.

ii. **Network Performance Management Tools (NPM)**

NPM tools are instrumental in monitoring the performance of a network of information technologies. To transform, in fact, a business often needs to rethink existing information systems or stretch its capacity near technical limits. There are always unexpected consequences when changes to IT systems occur; consequently, the tools to monitor their performances are a must. In detail, such systems should be able to monitor data flows, residual data storage capacity, percentage of internal CPU used by internal processes, and estimate the failure risks. These tools are essential because they may prevent catastrophic system failures that significantly delay digital transformation.

iii. **Advanced IT Analytics (AIA)**

AIAs enable managers to monitor the alignment between business and IT systems over time. These are, in fact, tools capable of simultaneously monitoring IT implementation advancements and their effects on value-creation activities at any level of the value stream. These tools may improve managers' awareness about areas that need intervention. In fact, these tools can help managers identify which new technologies are destroying value instead of creating it.

iv. **KPI to Monitor Advancements**

Many managers know the use of KPIs in any business transformation. Accordingly, it may still be useful in the management of digital transformation. KPIs considering IT implementation advancement status and time as variables can provide useful information about digital transformation processes' status. Obviously, such KPIs need to be considered holistically and may need to be used together simultaneously. Usually, KPI dashboards may help in this perspective. Dashboards are, in fact, graphical ensembles of various KPIs and may allow managers to observe more than one KPI simultaneously.

v. **Workspace Analytics**

Workspace analytics are tools that may allow managers to control the workload of each staff member. Additionally, such tools may enable managers to constantly monitor the principal difficulties all the staff members encounter. As any problem faced by a member of the staff may cause delays, with the help of these tools, managers may act promptly to help employees in need of solving their problem, and thus, digital transformation may continue to run.

vi. **Business Process Management Systems**

As assessed, any digital transformation endeavor should be based on smaller sequential processes. Indeed, it is only possible to change the whole business after some time. Therefore, the need to break the whole transformation into smaller processes emerged. Moving from these premises, it is clear why business process management systems are necessary to manage a digital transformation. Specifically, such a system may give managers an overall view of workload, system failure rates, task completion, and process standing. Such tools are also useful to evaluate the alignment between expectations and the real status of the transformation.

vii. **Automated Security Breach Detection Systems**

Data security is critical in the digital era. Indeed, if competitors may get their hands on your business data, they may know your future strategy. Next, customers' trust toward a digital technology tool may vary according to the perceived privacy protection ensured by the SME. Therefore, managers need to be capable of monitoring security breaches and eventual intrusions in business IT systems. Security breach detection systems may help managers solve this problem. Such tools, in fact, could inform managers if unauthorized users are accessing systems. Similarly, they could provide information concerning suspicious data movements from an internal database to an external database (i.e., by giving alerts informing of modifications or transfers of files).

As observed, tools are henceforth fundamental to managing digital transformation. However, such tools should be able to communicate with managers anytime. In fact, if a device can identify a problem but is incapable of expressing it, managers may not take any corrective action to solve it. Therefore, tools should also be capable of sending automatic alarms and alerts to all interested people. In this case, managers may receive the necessary information to properly manage the digital transformation and drive it to success.

6.2 Effective Strategies and Channels for SMEs

Our empirical findings demonstrate that channel marketing and distribution management are among the foremost elements to be changed during the digital transition. One of the most critical issues to be managed by SME marketers is the new 'phygital' approach increasingly required by the market and customers. Particularly referring to the food and wine case study, the founder of the SME clearly stated that providing products only through internet channels was not enough to sustain and defend their competitive advantage. Therefore, they decided immediately after the pandemic (2021) to open new physical temporary/pop-up stores where their loyal customers—but also new ones—might directly 'feel' the brand experience. The advantages in terms of customer satisfaction and retention are clear. Still, we also need to stress some critical issues, such as the risk of providing a 'physical' customer experience (i.e., in the offline store), which is perceived as very different with respect to the 'digital' experience. For SMEs wishing to move their marketing strategies toward I4.0, it is fundamental to create a seamless and consistent experience throughout all the channels, which is the key to success when opting for a transition from a conventional brick-and-mortar toward a click-and-mortar but also vice versa, as our findings suggest.

This consideration opens interesting streams for future research, both theoretical and practical, as our third case study on the fintech industry demonstrates. While digital and online channels are perfectly appropriate for SMEs starting their financial services in a technology-based perspective, the related possible strategies for a parallel physical marketing channel approach still need to be understood. Our suggestion, as agreed with the interviewees, is to always follow and respect a customer-centric approach by identifying the needs, expectations, and desires of the SME's targeted buyer persona. Marketers must remember that the risk of investing a high amount of money in a new digital channel is that customers might not appreciate several elements of the 'brand image' (i.e., from content to tone of voice), thus creating a brand image deterioration issue that might lead to loss of reputation.

Overall, notwithstanding the number of positive effects that digitalization of channels might provide to SMEs, managers and marketers should follow our hypothesized checklist framework (see Fig. 6.1) to make a careful step-by-step analysis of all the pros and cons that might emerge from the new digital channel.

6.3 Effects of 4.0 Marketing Strategies

Building on the empirical results of the previous section, we conceptualize a practical model (see Fig. 6.2) that attempts to answer some questions and critical issues derived from our interviews with managers and marketers of SMEs undergoing a digital transformation process. The model is in line with the step-by-step guide to digital transformation by

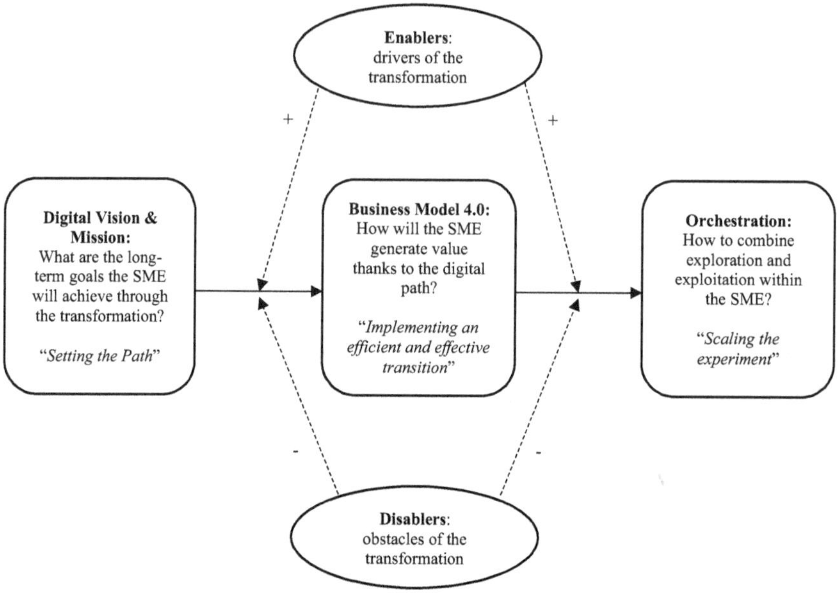

Fig. 6.2 Orchestrating an SME's digital transformation process. Source: Authors' elaboration

the World Economic Forum (2018), which stresses four main building blocks leading companies toward digital transformation, namely, (1) digital strategy, (2) business model, (3) enablers, and (4) orchestration.

Starting from left to right, the model (Fig. 6.2) begins with the first building block related to digital strategy, namely 'Digital Vision & Mission'. SME managers and marketers need to ask themselves before undergoing a digital transformation process, *what are the ultimate goals the company wants to achieve after the transition*? Moreover, *where do we want to strategically position the SME in the market*? In other words, this first step requires a clear and established roadmap that sets the 'digital path' in a consistent way with respect to the specific industry direction toward 4.0 marketing strategy implementation. Unfortunately, many SMEs start their digital path with no clear long-range planning or milestones to be achieved in the near and long future. It appears to be managers want to go digital just because the market requires them to do so. This is a big mistake every SME must avoid by, instead, setting a precise strategic vision and mission that needs to be appropriate not only with the industry's trends but most importantly with the company's identity.

The second and core building block of the model refers to business modeling. Precisely, value creation along the digital transition of the SME. Several elements of the company's ecosystem will positively (enablers) and negatively (disablers) impact the business performance during such a digital path. As previously stressed (see Fig. 6.1, element 6), monitoring and measuring through KPIs what the SME is accomplishing in each step of the digital transformation is essential. Using the appropriate resources (efficiency) to accomplish the predetermined goals (effectiveness) requires a trial-and-error approach (Kirk & Zollo, 2021). It is not possible that the digital path will be linear, with no mistakes or errors, which is why SME managers and marketers should be able to diagnose their oversights and learn from them in the future.

Among the main *enablers*—incentives and positive drivers—of business digitalization are (1) human capital, (2) holistic governance, (3) strategic partnerships, (4) customer-centric approaches, and (5) data management. In contrast, the main *disablers*—barriers hindering the digital path—that hinder the process are (6) lack of vision and mission, (7) resistance to change, (8) entrepreneurs' and managers' fear of the unknown and low-risk propensity, (9) rigid (non-agile) and inflexible (non-lean) organizational behavior, and (10) budget constraints.

Finally, we have *orchestration*, which refers to SMEs' management capability of adopting transformational leadership, holistic governance, funding and investor support, and community engagement. Without these elements, the digital path will remain a simple initial experiment. Instead, what SMEs want is a scalable digitalization of their business model able to simultaneously explore new mechanisms of creating value and, at the same time, exploit their conventional and (hopefully) successful way of doing business.

References

Amit, R., & Zott, C. (2015). Crafting business architecture: The antecedents of business model design. *Strategic Entrepreneurship Journal, 9*(4), 331–350.

Anderson, R. E., & Srinivasan, S. S. (2003). E-satisfaction and e-loyalty: A contingency framework. *Psychology & Marketing, 20*(2), 123–138.

Berman, S. J. (2012). Digital transformation: Opportunities to create new business models. *Strategy & Leadership, 40*(2), 16–24.

Caputo, A., Marzi, G., & Pellegrini, M. M. (2016). The internet of things in manufacturing innovation processes: Development and application of a conceptual framework. *Business Process Management Journal, 22*(2), 383–402.

Gambetti, R. C., & Graffigna, G. (2010). The concept of engagement: A systematic analysis of the ongoing marketing debate. *International Journal of Market Research, 52*(6), 801–826.

Hu, L., Filieri, R., Acikgoz, F., Zollo, L., & Rialti, R. (2022). The effect of utilitarian and hedonic motivations on mobile shopping outcomes. A cross-cultural analysis. *International Journal of Consumer Studies*. https://doi.org/10.1111/ijcs.12868

Jamali, D., Samara, G., Zollo, L., & Ciappei, C. (2020). Is internal CSR really less impactful in individualist and masculine Cultures? A multilevel approach. *Management Decision, 58*(2), 362–375.

Kane, G. C., Palmer, D., Phillips, A. N., Kiron, D., & Buckley, N. (2015). Strategy, not technology, drives digital transformation. *MIT Sloan Management Review and Deloitte University Press, 14*, 1–25.

Kirk, N. H., & Zollo, L. (2021). *European Venture Toolbox: The path for SMEs to grasp and defend opportunities*. Emerald Group Publishing.

Liang, T. P., & Tanniru, M. (2006). Customer-centric information systems. *Journal of Management Information Systems, 23*(3), 9–15.

Matt, C., Hess, T., & Benlian, A. (2015). Digital transformation strategies. *Business & Information Systems Engineering, 57*(5), 339–343.

Morey, T., Forbath, T., & Schoop, A. (2015). Customer data: Designing for transparency and trust. *Harvard Business Review, 93*(5), 96–105.

Parise, S., Guinan, P. J., & Kafka, R. (2016). Solving the crisis of immediacy: How digital technology can transform the customer experience. *Business Horizons, 59*(4), 411–420.

Pizzi, G., Scarpi, D., Pichierri, M., & Vannucci, V. (2019). Virtual reality, real reactions?: Comparing consumers' perceptions and shopping orientation across physical and virtual-reality retail stores. *Computers in Human Behavior, 96*, 1–12.

Quinton, S. (2013). The digital era requires new knowledge to develop relevant CRM strategy: A cry for adopting social media research methods to elicit this new knowledge. *Journal of Strategic Marketing, 21*(5), 402–412.

Rialti, R., Marzi, G., Ciappei, C., & Busso, D. (2019). Big data and dynamic capabilities: A bibliometric analysis and systematic literature review. *Management Decision*. https://doi.org/10.1108/MD-07-2018-0821

Setia, P., Setia, P., Venkatesh, V., & Joglekar, S. (2013). Leveraging digital technologies: How information quality leads to localized capabilities and customer service performance. *MIS Quarterly, 37*(2), 565–590.

Tallon, P. P., & Pinsonneault, A. (2011). Competing perspectives on the link between strategic information technology alignment and organizational agility: Insights from a mediation model. *MIS Quarterly, 35*(2), 463–486.

Wamba, S. F., & Mishra, D. (2017). Big data integration with business processes: A literature review. *Business Process Management Journal, 23*(3), 477–492.

Westerman, G., Bonnet, D., & McAfee, A. (2014b). The nine elements of digital transformation. *MIT Sloan Management Review, 7*, 1–6.

World Economic Forum. (2018). A step-by-step guide to digital transformation. Retrieved December 23, 2022, from https://www.weforum.org/agenda/2018/01/how-to-transform-a-company-into-a-digital-enterprise/

Zhu, K., Dong, S., Xu, S. X., & Kraemer, K. L. (2006). Innovation diffusion in global contexts: Determinants of post-adoption digital transformation of European companies. *European Journal of Information Systems, 15*(6), 601–616.

Zollo, L., Rialti, R., Tron, A., & Ciappei, C. (2021). Entrepreneurial passion, orientation and behavior: The moderating role of linear and nonlinear thinking styles. *Management Decision, 59*(5), 973–994.

7

Conclusion

The aim of the book was to identify the main paths that could make SMEs ready to thrive in the digital era by integrating 4.0 technologies into their marketing strategies. The starting point of the research was the identification of the importance of advanced digital technologies beyond the manufacturing realm. Henceforth, it was central first to deconstruct the meaning of the term digital in different areas and eras (Rialti et al., 2020).

It was thereby observed how the notion of digital technology evolved from the simple integration of computers within businesses in the third Industrial Revolution to the possibility during the fourth and current one to increasingly juxtapose automation to human workers to improve the way business processes are run. Digitally transforming the business thus means a complete revolution in the business, which provides a total change in the way SMEs operate, including the evaluation of the possibility of translating some activities from the real world to digital ones. A cultural revolution within the business is then necessary to completely benefit from digital technologies (Bag et al., 2021)

However, if a company is embracing emerging digital opportunities, several changes may occur within the business. The way companies develop and implement their marketing strategies will be affected

R. Rialti, L. Zollo, *Digital Transformation of SME Marketing Strategies*,
https://doi.org/10.1007/978-3-031-33646-1_7

dramatically (Krishen et al., 2021). Thanks to 4.0 technologies, it is in fact possible to develop new products capable of satisfying new customers, to better target these customers populating different virtual environments with respect to their predecessors, to improve their experience, and to improve the level of service the business could bring them.

Digital and digital technologies are therefore two buzzwords on the mouth of any manager around the world, and not considering the paradigmatic shift as something disruptive is a mistake that any manager should avoid, regardless of the size and industry of the business (Aversa et al., 2021).

While for large it is generically easier to implement digital technologies due to greater workforce expertise and resources, SMEs need to consider these technologies too (Scuotto et al., 2021). As stressed by the findings from three analyzed cases, thanks to 4.0 technologies, these businesses may achieve relevant strategic marketing objectives (De Luca et al., 2021). To summarize the findings emerging from the book, it is possible to observe how SMEs may:

1. get more data and insights about anything happening inside and around the business,
2. improve the strategic reach of the business in different markets,
3. identify and exploit innovative opportunities arising in the market,
4. detect, monitor, and engage different customers through digital touchpoints,
5. provide a greater quantity of information to any interested customer,
6. increase the level of service to customers,
7. create an immersive experience for customers,
8. develop new ad hoc or individual communication strategies,
9. develop more suitable pricing strategies capable,
10. better tie together production side and marketing side (i.e., for inventory and shipping management),
11. create new communication channels between employees/managers and customers,
12. exploiting the opportunities derived from B2B and B2C digital platforms.

The findings also show a possible path that may be followed by SMEs wishing to digitalize their marketing strategies, which consist of the following phases: (a) identifying who is leading the way, (b) making the case for digital transformation and crafting the vision within your business, (c) benchmarking current capabilities and defying resource requirements, (d) integrating new digital technologies into current systems and processes, (e) handling change management by managing culture, (f) measuring the outcomes, (g) not forgetting about customers, and (h) tools to manage the process. It was observed how the fifth and seventh phases are crucial in the transformation process.

During the fifth phase, in fact, it is necessary to consider the employees and to enact the procedures to involve the employees (or the whole organization) within the whole transformation process. In such a regard, the importance of first explaining to employees the benefits that the whole organization will obtain after the transformation in terms of competitiveness was thoroughly observed. Next, it is necessary to involve employees in how their work will change. As an example, it may be necessary to explain to employees that all the training to adopt a new technology may be fundamental to making their work easier, better, and perhaps funnier. The action that managers will have to undertake then concerns the development of commitment from the whole organization.

The seventh phase is likewise crucial. In such a phase, managers and directors must assess the reaction from consumers and take corrective actions that could influence the way the strategy will be corrected. Marketization provides in fact the total orientation of business to data to adjust marketing strategies. Thanks to data, businesses may develop a greater connection with customers and achieve new marketing objectives. In such a phase, data will drive the business toward new perspectives and toward more efficient marketing strategies.

Therefore, even for SMEs, it may be possible to develop 4.0-oriented marketing strategies. The effort may be great, but the efforts may be repaid according to possible achievable results.

What is missing is an understanding of the inner processes underlying the usage of data within the business. Likewise, customers may be fully satisfied with the complete satisfaction of SMEs or they may prefer human touch during an interaction (Kushwaha et al., 2021).

Such topics may be explored further, thus coping with the limitations of this research book and extending the literature. It is possible to suggest the exploration of these topics using quantitative assessment methods.

References

Aversa, J., Hernandez, T., & Doherty, S. (2021). Incorporating big data within retail organizations: A case study approach. *Journal of Retailing and Consumer Services, 60*, 102447.

Bag, S., Gupta, S., Kumar, A., & Sivarajah, U. (2021). An integrated artificial intelligence framework for knowledge creation and B2B marketing rational decision making for improving firm performance. *Industrial Marketing Management, 92*, 178–189.

De Luca, L. M., Herhausen, D., Troilo, G., & Rossi, A. (2021). How and when do big data investments pay off? The role of marketing affordances and service innovation. *Journal of the Academy of Marketing Science, 49*(4), 790–810.

Krishen, A. S., Dwivedi, Y. K., Bindu, N., & Kumar, K. S. (2021). A broad overview of interactive digital marketing: A bibliometric network analysis. *Journal of Business Research, 131*, 183–195.

Kushwaha, A. K., Kumar, P., & Kar, A. K. (2021). What impacts customer experience for B2B enterprises on using AI-enabled chatbots? Insights from Big data analytics. *Industrial Marketing Management, 98*, 207–221.

Rialti, R., Marzi, G., Caputo, A., & Mayah, K. A. (2020). Achieving strategic flexibility in the era of big data: The importance of knowledge management and ambidexterity. *Management Decision, 58*(8), 1585–1600.

Scuotto, V., Nicotra, M., Del Giudice, M., Krueger, N., & Gregori, G. L. (2021). A microfoundational perspective on SMEs' growth in the digital transformation era. *Journal of Business Research, 129*, 382–392.

References

Websites

https://www.apmdigest.com/digital-transformation-tools-1, Retrieved February 22, 2019.

https://bigdata-madesimple.com/top-business-intelligence-bi-tools-in-the-market/, Retrieved December 20, 2018.

https://www.forbes.com/sites/barbarathau/2017/05/15/is-the-rfid-retail-revolution-finally-here-a-macys-case-study/#107b3e543294, Retrieved February 20, 2019.

https://www.forbes.com/sites/kashmirhill/2012/02/16/how-target-figured-out-a-teen-girl-was-pregnant-before-her-father-did/#370aa55a6668, Retrieved February 19, 2019.

https://www.futurelearn.com/courses/digital-skills-web-analytics, Retrieved October 14, 2018.

https://www.ikea.com/ms/en_US/this-is-ikea/ikea-highlights/Virtual-reality/index.html, Retrieved October 14, 2018.

https://optinmonster.com/ecommerce-personalization-examples/, Retrieved February 14, 2019.

R. Rialti, L. Zollo, *Digital Transformation of SME Marketing Strategies*,
https://doi.org/10.1007/978-3-031-33646-1

https://www.ibm.com/analytics/hadoop/big-data-analytics, Retrieved February 20, 2019.

https://www.scaleoutsoftware.com/technology/how-object-oriented-programming-simplifies-data-parallel-analytics/, Retrieved December 20, 2018.

https://smartereum.com/7630/how-alibaba-is-championing-the-application-of-blockchain-technology-in-china-and-beyond-wed-feb-20/, Retrieved December 10, 2018.

https://www.shopify.com/retail/how-these-retailers-are-using-augmented-reality-to-enhance-the-customer-experience, Retrieved February 20, 2019.

https://www.techemergence.com/artificial-intelligence-retail/, Retrieved October 14, 2018.

https://kontakt.io/beacon-basics/what-is-a-beacon/, Retrieved October 14, 2018.

https://blog.hubspot.com/marketing/iot-retail, Retrieved October 14, 2018.

https://www.techrepublic.com/article/how-to-create-a-vision-for-digital-transformation-at-your-company/, Retrieved December 28, 2018.

https://www.inc.com/jason-albanese/these-4-companies-have-been-saved-by-digital-transformation.html, Retrieved October 14, 2018.

Index

R. Rialti, L. Zollo, *Digital Transformation of SME Marketing Strategies*,
https://doi.org/10.1007/978-3-031-33646-1

I

M

S

T

V

Kolibri 360 GmbH
Ferdinand-Jühlke-Straße 7
99095 Erfurt, Deutschland
produktsicherheit@kolibri360.de